Kid's Box

American English

Starter Teacher's Resource Book

with Online Audio

Second Edition

Kathryn Escribano

with Caroline Nixon & Michael Tomlinson

CAMBRIDGE
UNIVERSITY PRESS

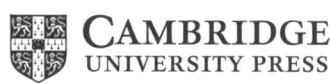

CAMBRIDGE
UNIVERSITY PRESS

University Printing House, Cambridge CB2 8BS, United Kingdom

Cambridge University Press is part of the University of Cambridge.

It furthers the University's mission by disseminating knowledge in the pursuit of education, learning and research at the highest international levels of excellence.

www.cambridge.org
Information on this title: www.cambridge.org/9781107431027

© Cambridge University Press 2015

It is normally necessary for written permission for copying to be obtained in advance from a publisher. The worksheets in this book are designed to be copied and distributed in class.
The normal requirements are waived here and it is not necessary to write to Cambridge University Press for permission for an individual teacher to make copies for use within his or her own classroom. Only those pages that carry the wording '© Cambridge University Press' may be copied.

First published 2015

Printed in China by Golden Cup Printing Co. Ltd

A catalogue record for this publication is available from the British Library

ISBN 978-1-107-43102-7 Teacher's Resource Book with Online Audio Starter
ISBN 978-1-107-43099-0 Class Book Starter with CD-ROM
ISBN 978-1-107-43157-7 Teacher's Book Starter
ISBN 978-1-107-43100-3 Class Audio CDs Starter (2 CDs)
ISBN 978-1-107-43103-4 Flashcards Starter (pack of 78)
ISBN 978-1-107-69025-7 Interactive DVD with Teacher's Booklet Starter
ISBN 978-1-107-43108-9 Presentation Plus Starter
ISBN 978-1-107-43109-6 Posters Starter

Additional resources for this publication at www.cambridge.org/elt/kidsboxamericanenglish

Cambridge University Press has no responsibility for the persistence or accuracy of URLs for external or third-party internet websites referred to in this publication, and does not guarantee that any content on such websites is, or will remain, accurate or appropriate.

Contents

Introduction	4
Record sheet	5
Teacher's notes and worksheets	
Unit 1: Hi!	6
Unit 2: My class	12
Unit 3: My colors	18
Unit 4: My toys	24
Unit 5: My house	30
Unit 6: My body	36
Unit 7: My animals	42
Unit 8: My food	48
Worksheet covers	54

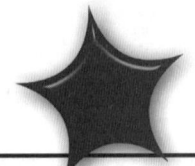

Introduction

- This Teacher's Resource Book is designed to help you and your students make the most of *Kid's Box Starter*. For each unit of the Class Book, you will find two reinforcement worksheets and two extension worksheets. The former are designed to help those students who need extra practice, whereas the latter are designed to cater to the needs of fast finishers. However, these worksheets not only provide a resource for mixed-ability classes, but also offer material for the rest of the class to use while you work individually with a student.

- Reinforcement worksheets 1 and 2 for each unit focus on key vocabulary, as does Extension worksheet 1. Extension worksheet 2 offers further exploitation of the story in each unit. The audio for these activities is to be found online on the *Kid's Box* website. We recommend you use audio to help your students get used to a variety of voices.

- There is also a Song worksheet for each unit. These offer a song-based activity, which varies from unit to unit. These worksheets are best done once students are familiar with the song. The songs are provided online on the *Kid's Box* website but you can also use the Class Audio CDs. Please note that the audio track numbers refer to the *Kid's Box American English Starter Teacher's Resource Book Online Audio*. You may like to photocopy and laminate these song worksheets and put them up on the wall as you complete each unit. Then, in future lessons, when you need to fill time, you can ask a student to point to one of these worksheets and then play/sing that song again.

- There is a page of teaching notes before the worksheets for each unit. These notes include optional follow-up activities that encourage class interaction and add an extra dimension to each worksheet. You may find that one type of follow-up activity works better than another with a particular class, in which case you can use the suggestion as a springboard for adapting other worksheets.

- You may find, according to the particular interests of each student, that in one unit he/she needs a reinforcement worksheet, whereas in other units, the same student can more profitably do an extension worksheet. Fast finishers may want/need to do both reinforcement and extension worksheets.

- Bear in mind that with students of this age, fast finishers are not always the students who have better understood the new language. Encourage your students to take pride in their work rather than rush to finish it. You may want to praise students who have done the worksheet particularly carefully in order to make this a model to aspire to.

- You can also use the worksheets when you need to fill time or as alternative activities when, for example, some other activity (a whole-school project, a field trip, a holiday, etc.) has interfered with the normal running of the class.

- You may like to give these worksheets to students as they do them or you may like to keep them together to bind them at the end of the semester/year. If you decide to do this, you can photocopy the cover pages on pages 54 and 55 of this Teacher's Resource Book.

- In addition, you can use pages 54 and 55 as review worksheets. Use them as a color dictation, e.g., *Color the couch green* or ask, e.g., *How many robots can you see?, Is the dog under the bed or on the bed?*

- You may find it useful to keep a record of the unit worksheets each student has completed. To do this, you can photocopy the record sheet on the next page for each unit.

Name	Reinforcement worksheet 1	Reinforcement worksheet 2	Extension worksheet 1	Extension worksheet 2	Song worksheet

Teacher's notes

Reinforcement worksheet 1

- Students look at the characters and say their correct names. Students then color in the characters and the backgrounds. They cut them out and use them as bookmarks. See also Extension worksheet 2, *Optional follow-up activity*.

- *Optional follow-up activity:* Students work in pairs, A and B. Student A lifts up one of the bookmarks, and Student B says *Hi* to the character, e.g., *Hi, Marie!* Students A and B exchange roles.

- *Optional audio activity:* Play the audio (Track 2). As they listen, students lift the character who has been named and repeat the greeting.

Key: 1 Hi, Marie! 2 Hi, Monty! 3 Hi, Marie! 4 Hi, Maskman! 5 Hi, Maskman! 6 Hi, Monty!

Reinforcement worksheet 2

- Students look at the faces and use their fingers to trace over the example. They then use a pencil to draw the noses. When they have drawn all six, they color in the faces and add hair. Encourage them to be original!

- *Optional follow-up activity:* Students work in pairs, A and B. Student A points to a face, and Student B says the number. Students A and B exchange roles.

- As part of your assembly routine, when you count how many students are absent, you can draw (or ask a student to draw) the number face on the board.

- *Optional audio activity:* Play the audio (Track 3). As they hear a number, students find the face and trace over the number with their fingers.

Key: 5, 2, 3, 6, 1, 4.

Extension worksheet 1

- Copy onto thin cardboard for best results. Students color and cut out the birthday scene and the number wheel. Help them cut out the shaded area in the birthday scene. Help students fix the number wheel to the back of the cardboard using a round head fastener. Push this through the cross in the birthday scene and then through the cross in the middle of the number wheel. If it is easier, students can use a pencil to make the holes. Say a number. Students move the number wheel so that the number is showing. Ask *How old are you?* Students answer with the visible number. They then repeat the exercise in pairs.

- *Optional follow-up activity:* Students choose a number and move the number wheel accordingly. Say, e.g., *I'm three. If your number is three, stand up.* Repeat with other numbers.

Extension worksheet 2

- Students look at the pictures. They listen to the story frame by frame (Track 4) and point to the picture that goes with it. As they hear each frame, students write the number in the correct picture. Play the audio again so they can follow the story.

Key: 2, 5, 3, 6, 4, 1.

- *Optional follow-up activity:* Students can use the characters from Reinforcement worksheet 1. Divide the class into three groups and give each group one of the three cutout characters. Play the story. Students in each group lift their character when their character speaks.

Song worksheet

- Prepare a set of cards in advance. Show one of the owls and ask *How old are you?* Imitate the owl's answer, e.g., *I'm five.* Repeat with another number, then give the remaining cards to four students and ask them to answer with the age of the owl they are holding. Take the cards back and fix them to the board. One of them should be face down (so that the image is hidden). Point to the hidden owl and ask *How old are you?* Students look at the remaining owls. They figure out the age of the hidden owl and answer. Students sing the song (Track 5), pointing to each answering owl on their worksheets.

- *Optional follow-up activity:* Students decorate and cut out the cards. Students work in pairs, A and B. Student A points to one of the owls and asks *How old are you?* Student B answers. Students A and B exchange roles.

Unit 1 Reinforcement worksheet 1

 Look, color, and cut.

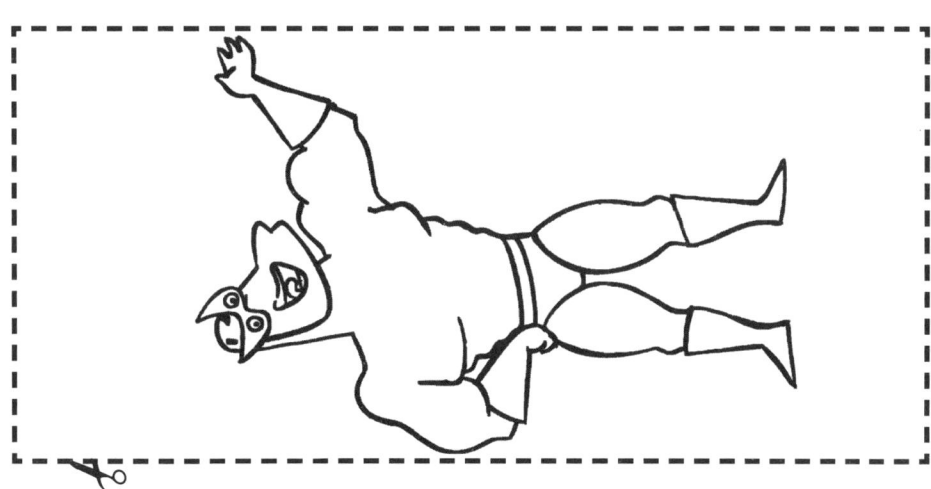

Unit 1 Reinforcement Worksheet 2

Trace and color.

Extension worksheet 1

  Make and play.

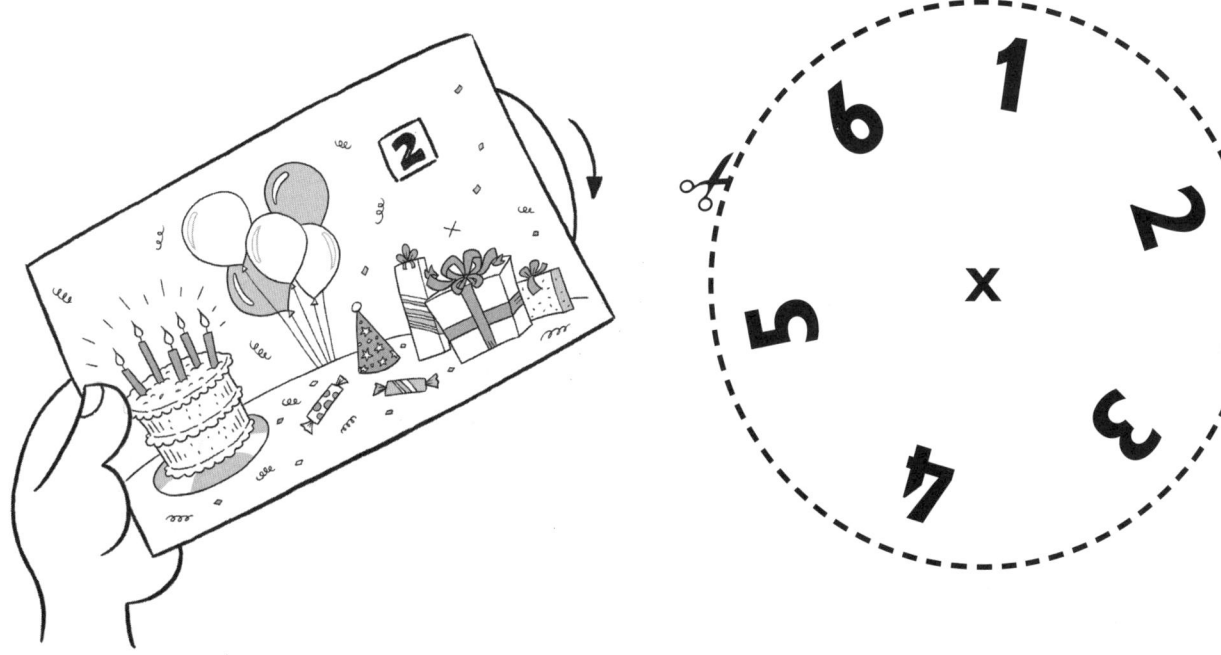

Unit 1 Extension worksheet 2

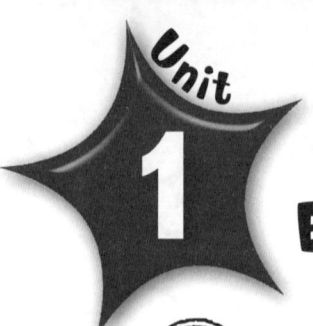

Listen, point, and write.

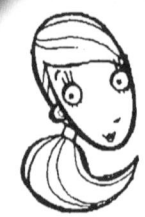

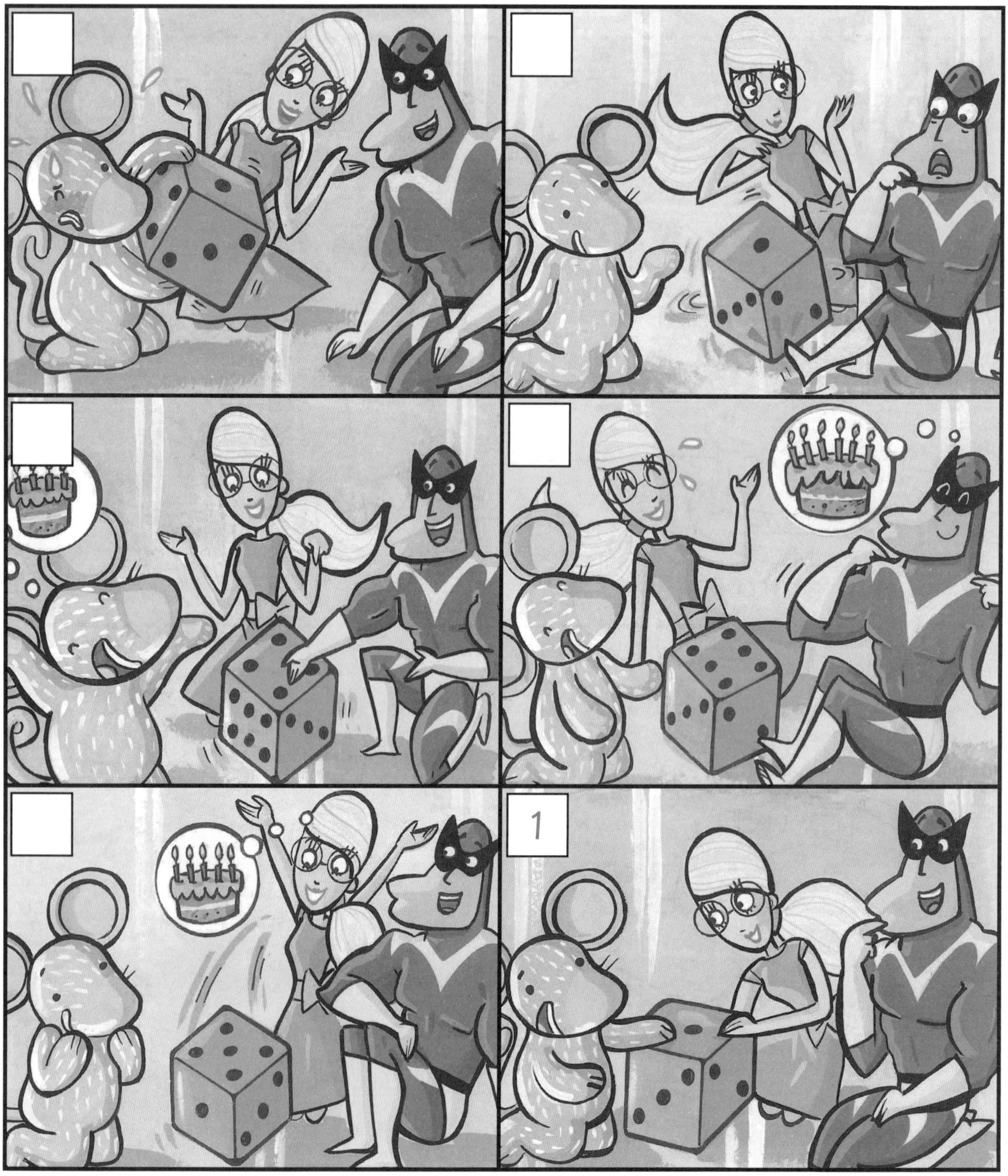

Song worksheet

   Play, point, and sing.

2 Teacher's notes

Reinforcement worksheet 1

- Students decorate and color the bag. Encourage them to be creative and to use different patterns and colors. Students cut out the bag. Show them how to fold over the flap to make a pocket. Use staples or Scotch tape to fasten the sides of the flap into place, being careful to leave a space at the top for students to insert the objects. Students color the flap. Students then color and cut out the objects and put them into the pocket.
- Students work in pairs, A and B. Student A names one of the objects, and Student B puts it into the pocket. Students A and B exchange roles.
- *Optional follow-up activity:* Students work in small groups. The rest of the group close their eyes, while Student A puts only four objects into the pocket. The other students have to guess which object is missing and lay their guess on the desk hidden under their hand. Student A names each object as he/she takes it out. If a student has the named object under his/her hand, he/she is "out." The winner is the student whose object is not named.
- *Optional audio activity:* Students listen to the audio (Track 6). Students place the objects in the pocket as they are named. Check they are doing this correctly.

Key: pencil, book, chair, eraser, table.

Reinforcement worksheet 2

- Students look at the classroom scene and count how many pictures there are of each object. Guide students through the example by getting them to find and circle all five pencils. They write the numbers in the boxes. Students then color in the scene.
- Students work in pairs, A and B. Student A says a number, and Student B says the name of the corresponding object(s). Students A and B exchange roles.
- *Optional follow-up activity:* Students work in small groups. One student asks *What's this?* and starts to draw one of the classroom objects. The first to guess the correct object is the next to draw. To extend this activity, Student A gives his/her picture to another member of the group and asks *Where's this?* Student B points to the object on the worksheet.

- *Optional audio activity:* Students listen to the audio (Track 7) and check their answers.

Key: 5 pencils, 4 books, 3 erasers, 6 bags, 2 tables, 6 chairs.

Extension worksheet 1

- Copy onto thin cardboard for best results. Students color and cut out the spinner. Help them make a hole in the center of the spinner and show them how to push a pencil through it. Demonstrate how to play *Spin the spinner* by doing the action that the spinner lands on. Students spin their spinners and do the actions. They can record their game in the chart by crossing out a number each time they land on that particular action. Ask students which action was first to reach six spins.
- *Optional follow-up activity:* In pairs, both students spin their spinners. If the two spinners land on the same action, students both name the action and do it together; if different, they each say their action but do not do it.

Extension worksheet 2

- Students look at the frames and remember the story. They circle the image they think is missing from each frame. They then listen to the story (Track 8) and check their answers.

Key: 1 A, 2 A, 3 B, 4 A, 5 B, 6 B.

- Check students' answers, then ask them to draw in the missing objects.
- *Optional follow-up activity:* Point to frame one. Say *Two ch...* to elicit chairs. Do the same with the objects in the other frames (*three er... , four p... , five b...*). Students can also do this in pairs.

Song worksheet

- Prepare a set of cards in advance on thin cardboard for best results. Shuffle the cards. As you show the class each card, give instructions, e.g., *Maskman says stand up!* Then give an instruction without the words *Maskman says*. Whoever carries out the action is eliminated.
- Play the song (Track 9). Students join in with the actions.
- *Optional follow-up activity:* Students cut out their own sets of cards and play in groups. They take turns giving instructions.

Unit 2 Reinforcement worksheet 1

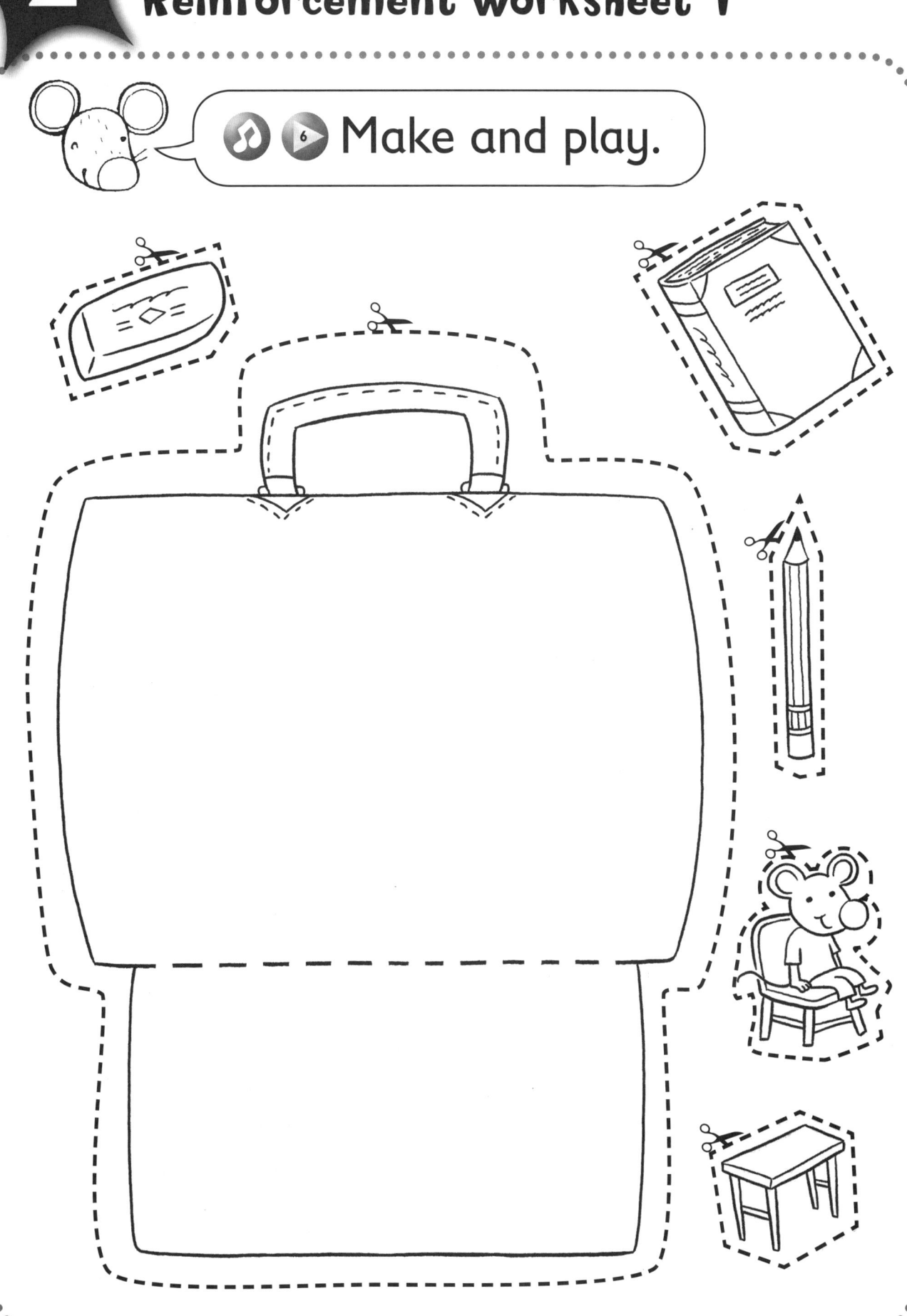

Make and play.

Unit 2 — Reinforcement worksheet 2

Count. Write the number.

Unit 2

Extension worksheet 1

Make and play.

1 2 3 4 5 6	1 2 3 4 5 6	1 2 3 4 5 6	1 2 3 4 5 6	1 2 3 4 5 6	1 2 3 4 5 6	1 2 3 4 5 6

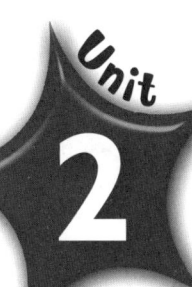

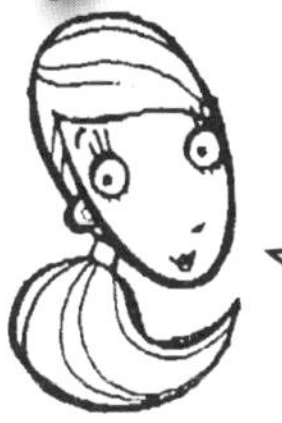

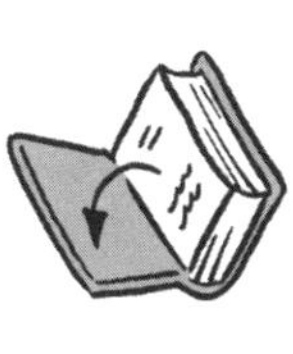

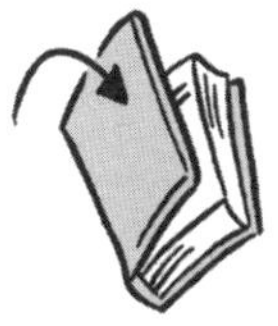

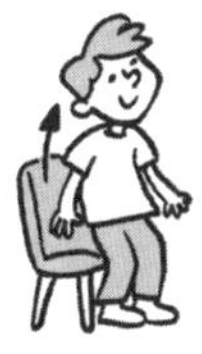

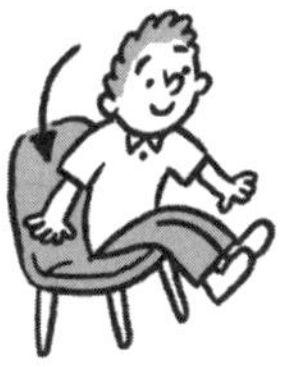

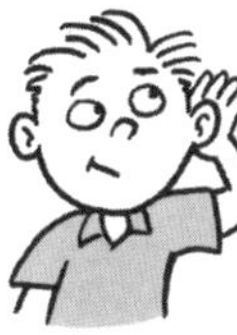

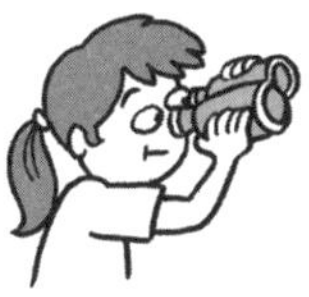

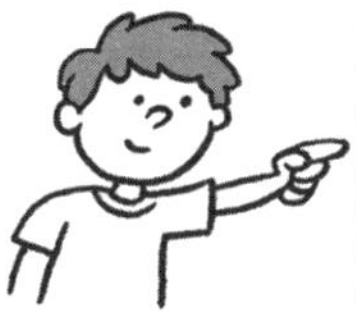

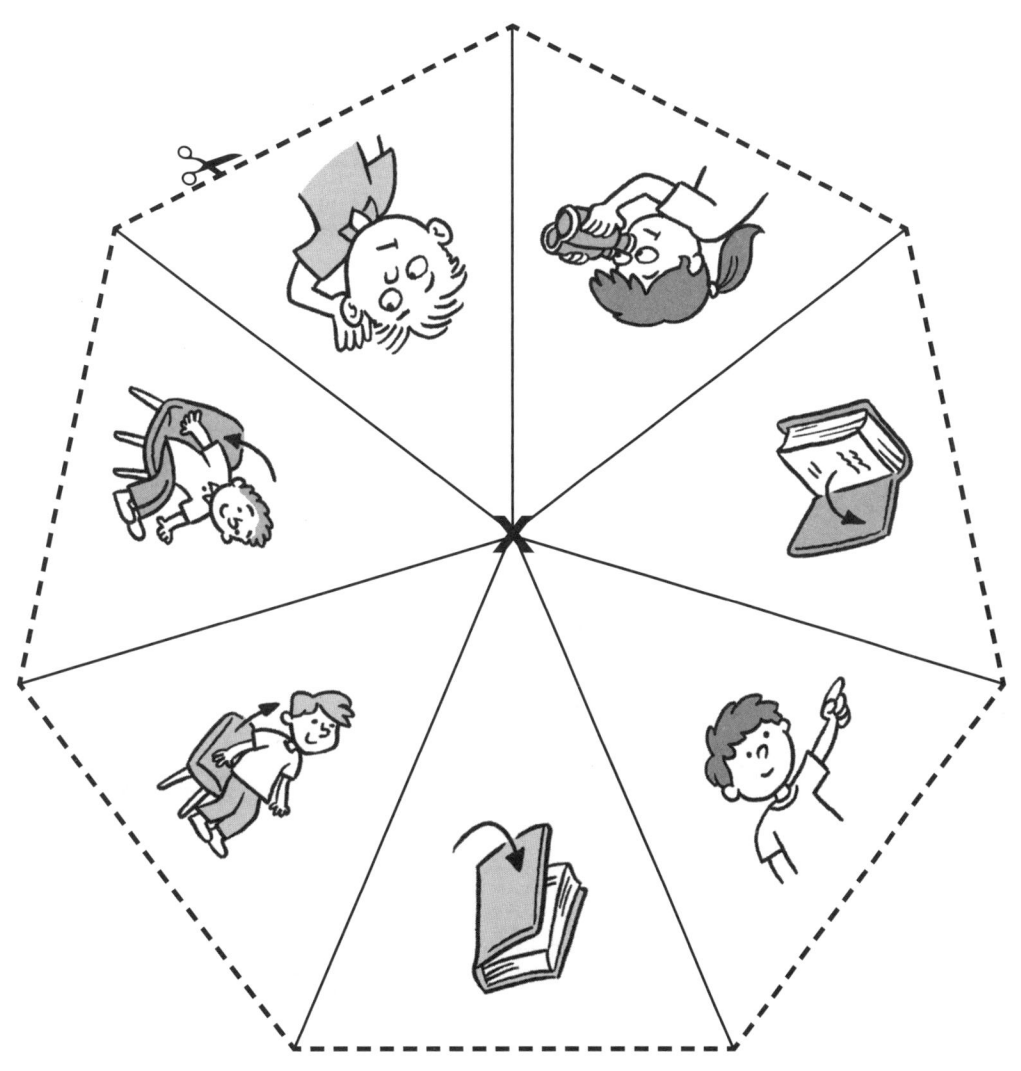

Extension worksheet 2

  Think and circle. Listen.

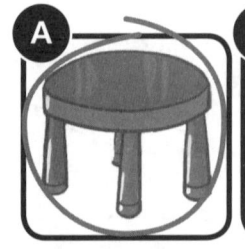  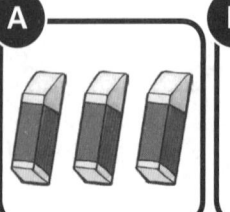 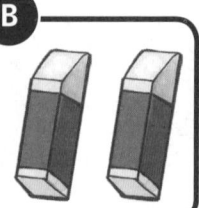 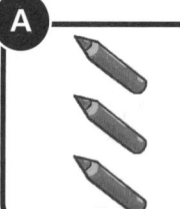 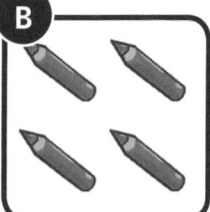

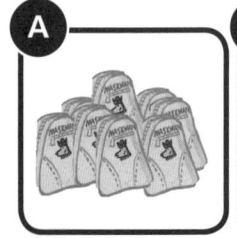  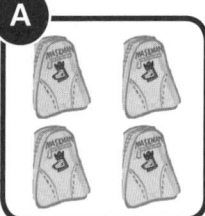 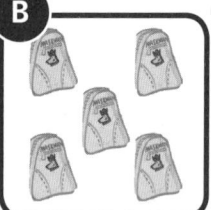 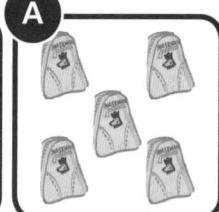 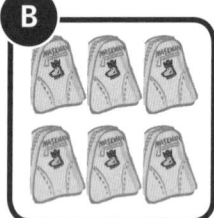

 Think and draw.

Unit 2

Song worksheet

  Play and sing.

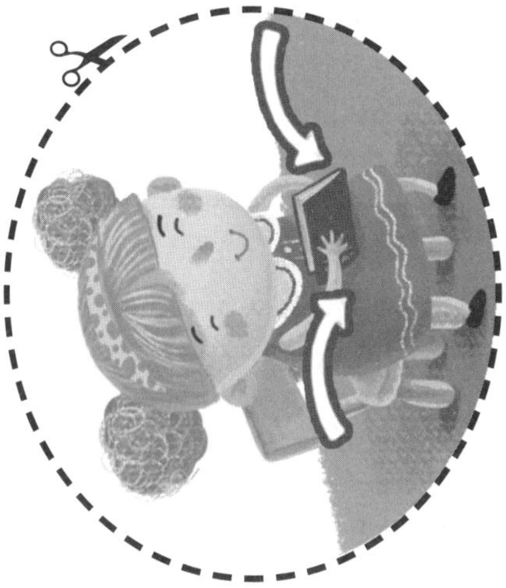

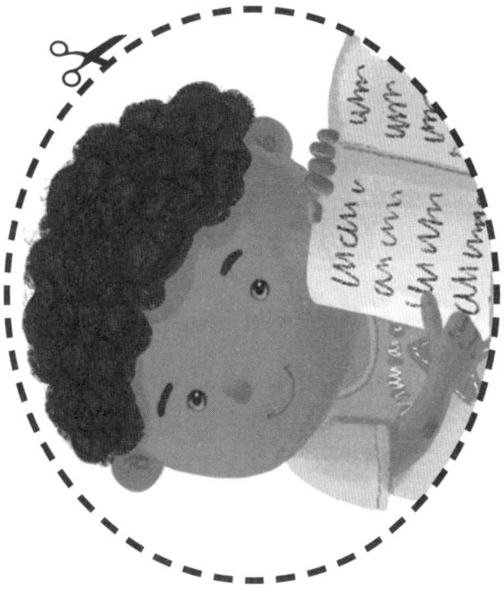

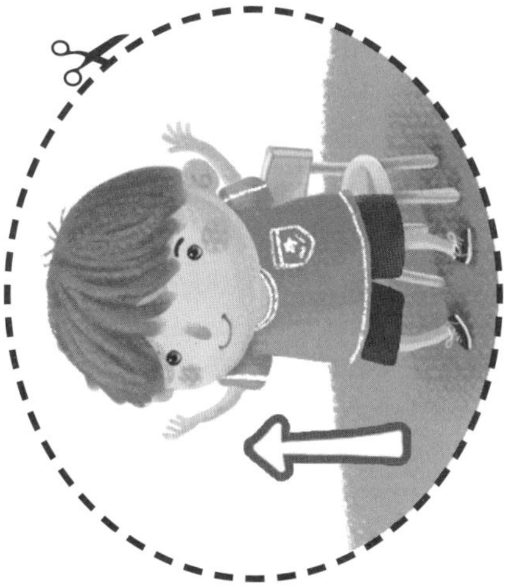

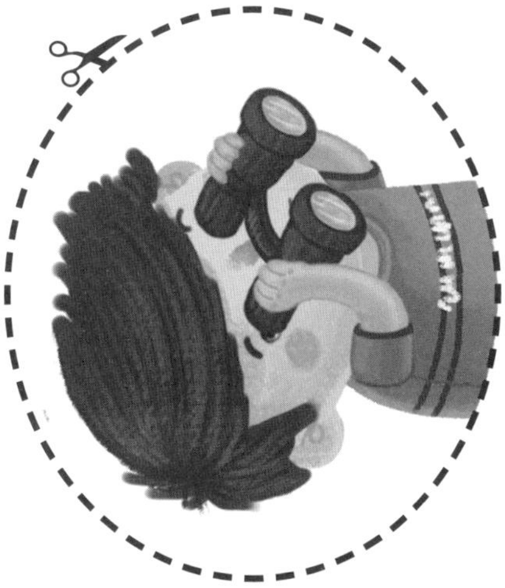

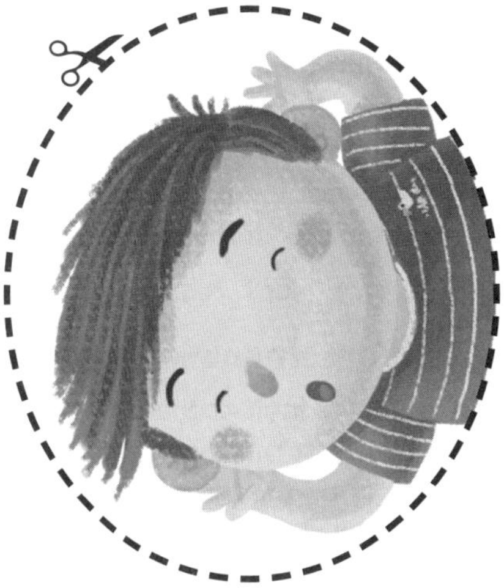

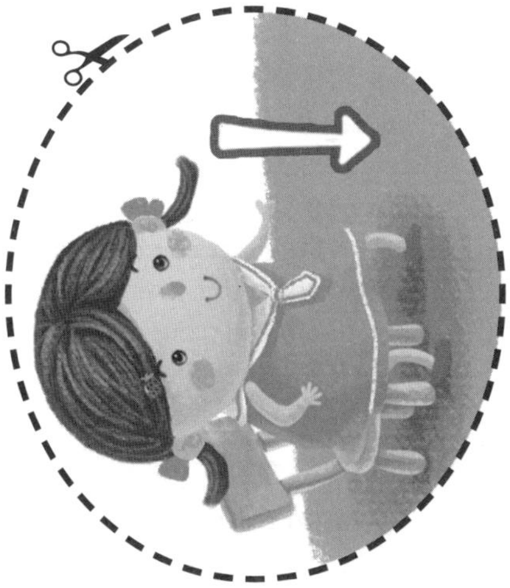

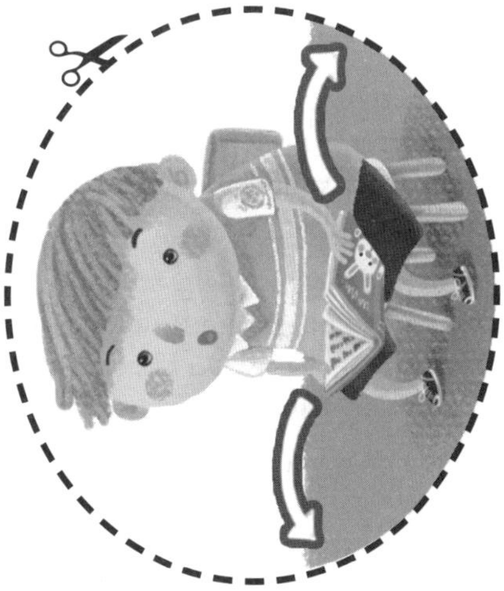

3 Teacher's notes

Reinforcement worksheet 1

- Copy onto thin cardboard for best results. Students color each paint splash a different color (*red, white, yellow, brown, black, blue*). They cut out and separate the A cards from the B cards. They lay them face down in rows and then turn over one card from each row to form color pairs. When they form a pair, e.g., the two blue halves, they name the color.

- *Optional follow-up activity:* Give students long strips of paper and ask them to glue the complete splashes to the paper in order of preference, putting their favorite color at the top and their least favorite at the bottom. Students work in pairs, A and B. Student A tells Student B the order of their colors. Student B then does the same.

- To extend this activity, all students stand up. A student says his/her favorite color. Students who have the same favorite color remain standing. The rest sit down. The student then says his/her second favorite color. Again, those who prefer the same color remain standing and the rest sit down. This continues until all six colors have been named.

- *Optional audio activity:* Alternatively, students listen to the audio (Track 10) and color in the paint splashes. Ask them to lift up each crayon before coloring so you can check they have chosen the right color. They then continue with the rest of the activity.

Key: blue, black, red, white, yellow, brown.

Reinforcement worksheet 2

- Students look at the classroom objects in the thought bubbles at the top of the page. Put flashcards of the six colors on the board. Ask students to vote on the color of each classroom object. Say *What color is the pencil?* The color with most votes is used to color the pencil. Remove this color flashcard from the board. Continue until students have colored all the classroom objects.

- *Optional follow-up activity:* Students then draw the objects in each character's transparent shopping bag, following the example, and color the objects the same color as in the thought bubbles.

- *Optional audio activity:* Alternatively, students listen to the audio (Track 11) and point to each object as it is named. Ask *What color is the pencil?* Do the same for the other objects. Students decide and color the objects.

Key: pencil, bag, eraser, book, chair, table.

Extension worksheet 1

- Copy onto thin cardboard for best results. Students color each oval with one of the colors from the unit, then cut them out. They lay the strips one on top of the other and use a round head fastener to join them together to make a fan.

- Students work in pairs, A and B. Student A asks Student B *What's your favorite color?* Student B separates out the color from the fan and says *My favorite color's ...* . Students A and B exchange roles.

- In groups, one student asks the student on his/her left *What's your favorite color?* When he/she answers, all the students separate out the color. Play continues until all the students have asked and answered.

- *Optional follow-up activity:* Students use a sheet of paper and their favorite colors to design a class flag. Show the class the completed flags and ask them to guess whose each flag is.

Extension worksheet 2

- Do a color dictation. Say *Color number one, blue!* Students color the paint splash on paintbrush 1, blue. Do the same with 2 – red, 3 – black, 4 – white, 5 – brown, and 6 – yellow. Students then use this code to color in the picture at the bottom of the page. Explain that mail boxes are red in the United Kingdom.

- Students listen to the story (Track 12) and check the box below each paintbrush if that color is mentioned in the story. They listen to the story again and check their answers.

Key: There should be check marks below every paintbrush except 5 – brown.

- *Optional follow-up activity:* A student comes to the front of the class and closes his/her eyes with the six color flashcards beside him/her. Count around the class, pointing to a student for each word of the unit 3 chant. When you say the final *white*, the student you are pointing to chooses a flashcard from the front of the class and hides it behind his/her back. The student at the front looks at the flashcards and says which one is missing. The student with the missing flashcard is next to come to the front.

Song worksheet

- Ask students to remember the color of each object in the song. Ask them to hold their colored pencil in the air so that you can check before they color the card for each object. Students can also color the troll cards the same color to help them remember. Students cut out the cards and match the trolls with the objects. As they sing the song (Track 13), they lift the correct troll and object for each verse.

Key: brown chair, white eraser, blue table, red pencil.

- *Optional follow-up activity:* In pairs, students play with both sets of cards. They shuffle and deal the cards and use them to play *Snap*. At the same time, both students lay a card face up on the desk. When both lay the same card, they have to say *Snap!* The first student to say *Snap!* takes all the cards in the pile. Play continue until a student has won all the cards.

Unit 3 — Reinforcement worksheet 1

Make and play.

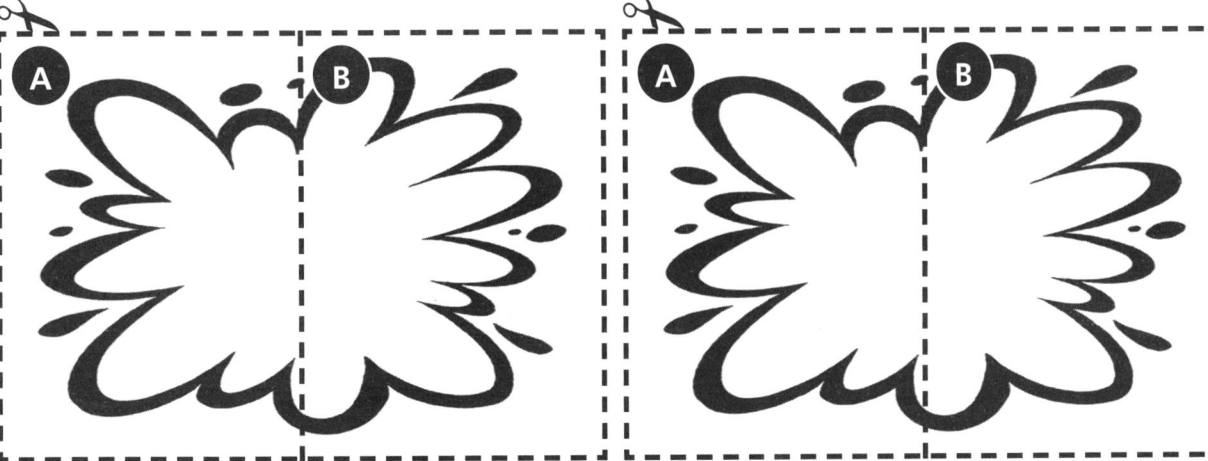

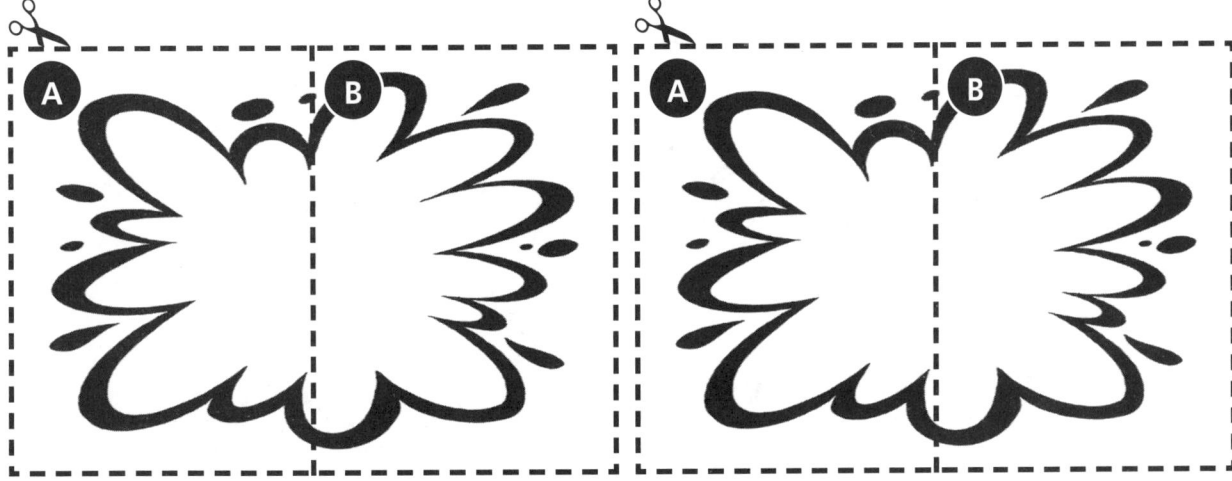

Unit 3 Reinforcement worksheet 2

Think and color. Draw.

Unit 3

Extension worksheet 1

  Make and play.

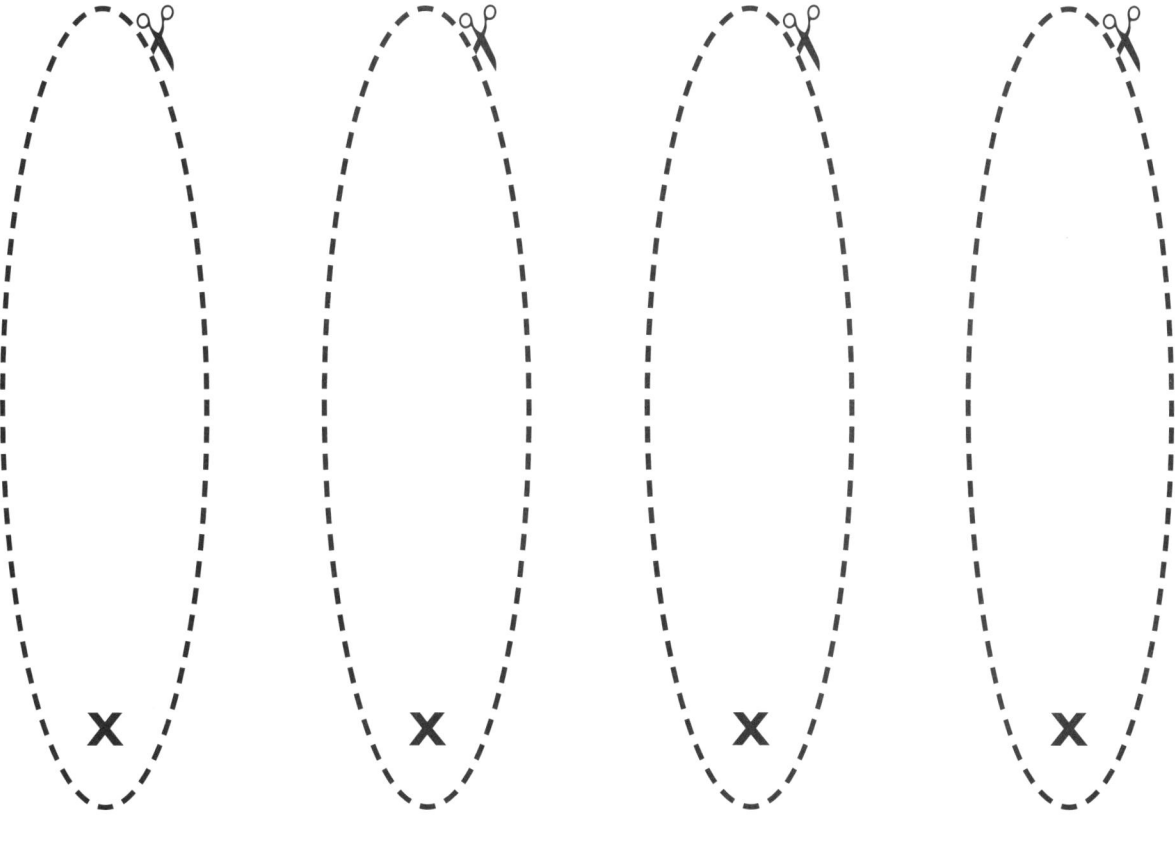

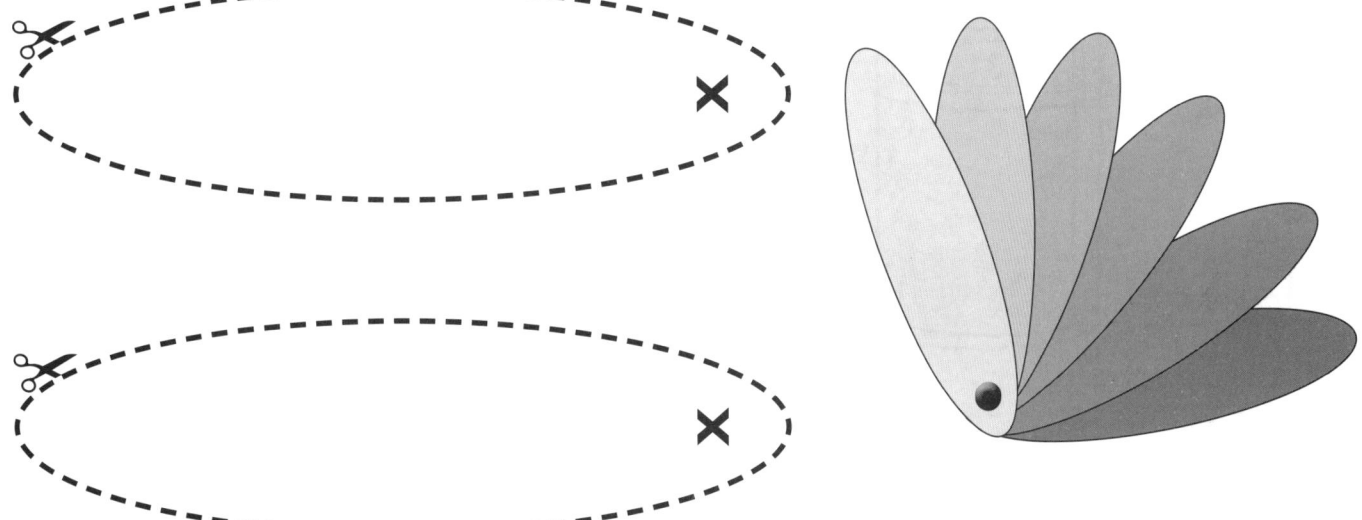

Extension worksheet 2

  Color. Listen and check (✓).

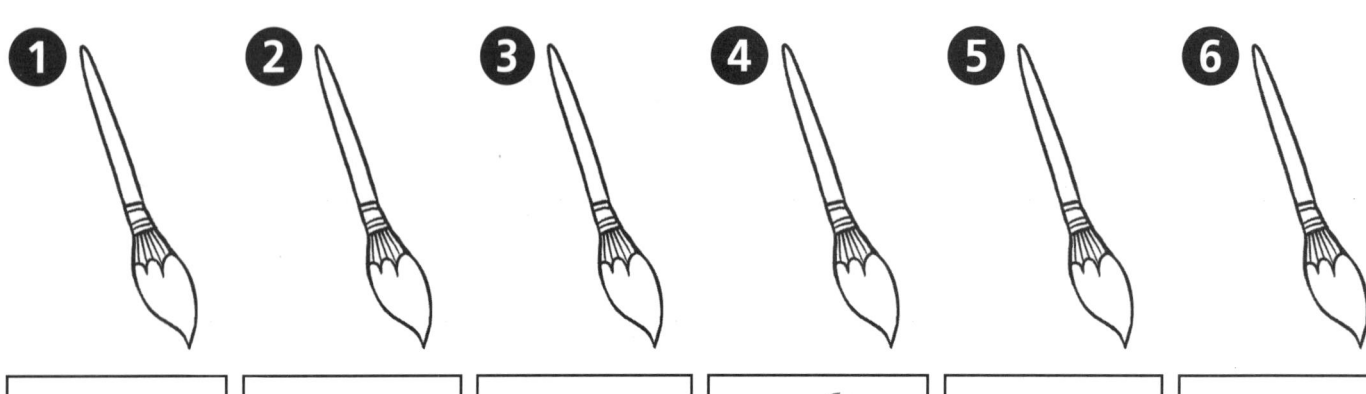

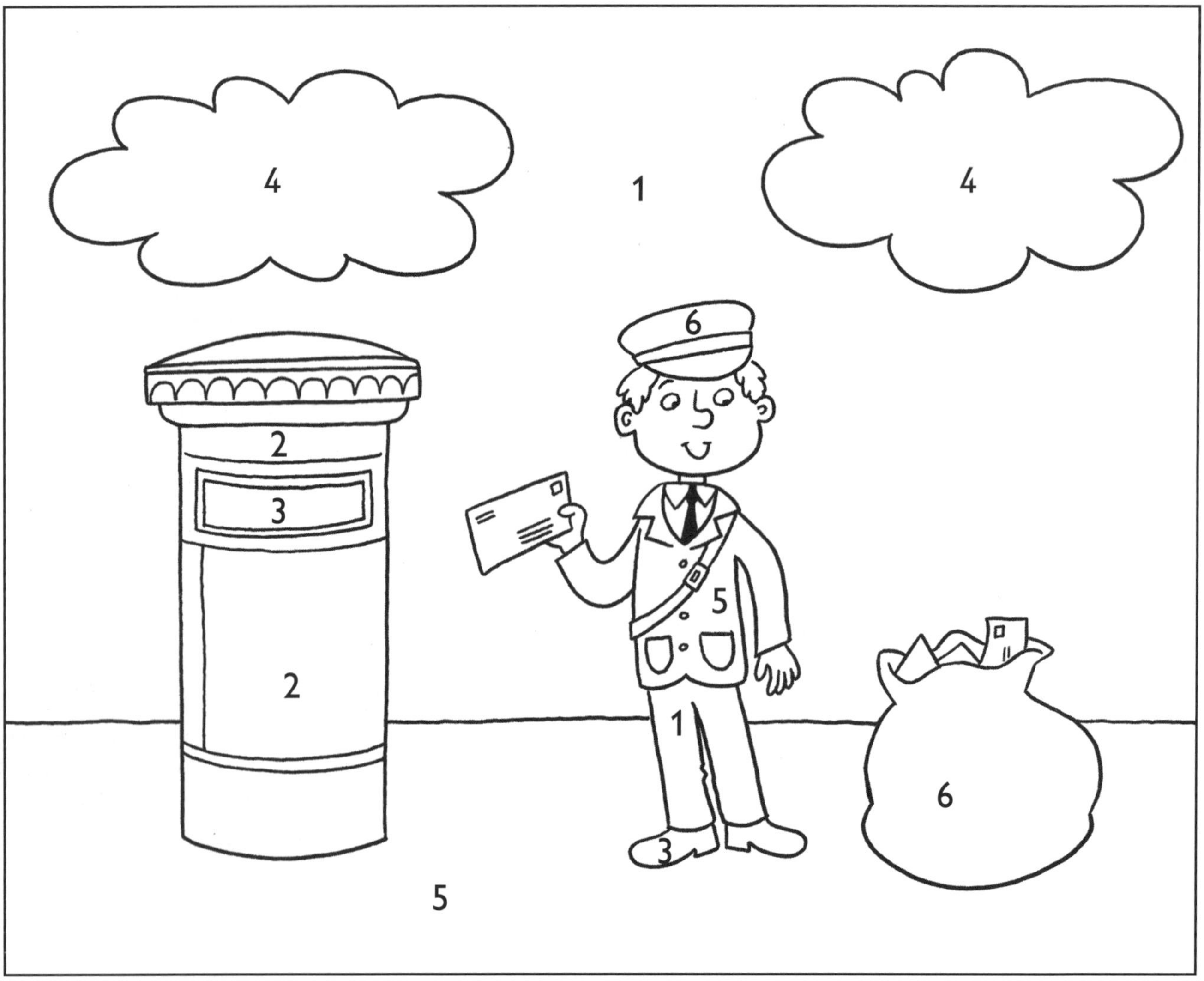

Unit 3

Song worksheet

   Think and color. Sing.

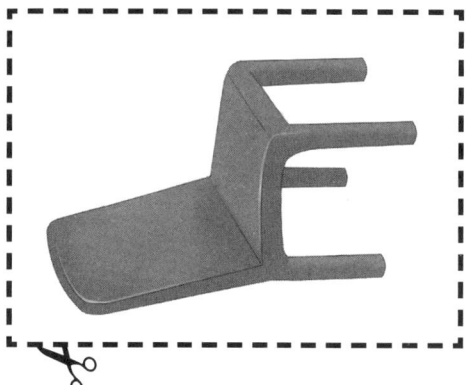

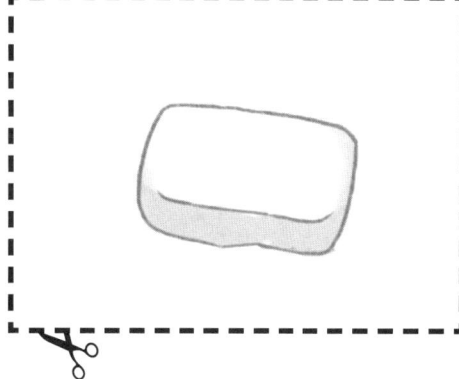

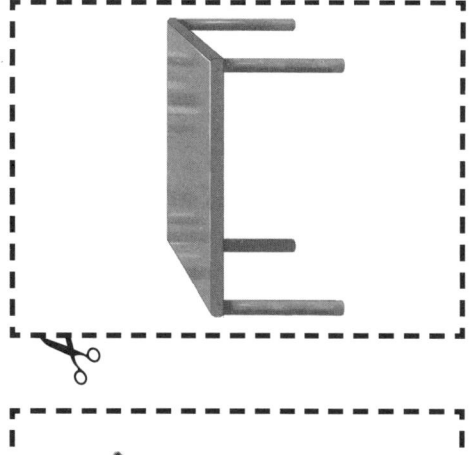

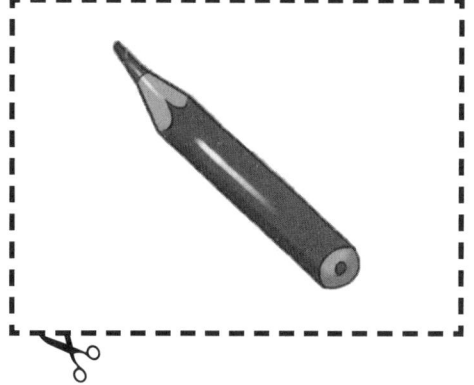

4 Teacher's notes

Reinforcement worksheet 1

- Students cover the bottom half of the page with their exercise books. They look at the outlines and guess what each object is. Then they uncover the page and use a pencil to follow the dotted lines going from each object to its partner in the scene. They color in the objects, using one color for each. When students have finished coloring in the toys, do a class survey of which colors were used for which object, e.g., *Hands up if your robot is brown!* and count the number of students. Students then color the rest of the scene.

- *Optional follow-up activity:* Alternatively, students use modeling clay to make a ball and a robot. They describe what they have made, e.g., *a yellow and brown ball.*

- *Optional audio activity:* Alternatively, students follow the dotted lines as the objects are named in the audio (Track 14). Make sure they are all pointing to the right object before they color them in (with colors of their choice).

Key: bike, doll, car, ball, robot, kite.

Reinforcement worksheet 2

- Copy onto thin cardboard for best results. Do a color dictation. Ask students to look at the spinner and say *Color the robot yellow,* etc. (see Key below). Continue until students have colored each object correctly.

- Students cut out the spinner. Help them push a pencil through the center. They spin the spinner six times, coloring each numbered section of the kite the color of the toy that the spinner lands on, e.g., if with the first spin the spinner lands on the car, which is red, they color section 1 of the kite red, etc. Display the kites. Students choose their favorite.

- *Optional follow-up activity:* Decide on an action for each toy, e.g., bouncing the ball, rocking the doll. Students work in pairs, A and B. Student A spins the spinner, and Student B does the action. Students A and B exchange roles.

- *Optional audio activity:* Students listen to the audio (Track 15) and lay that side of the spinner on the desk. Check students' answers.

Key: a red car, a yellow robot, a black ball, a blue bike, a brown doll.

Extension worksheet 1

- Students color the scene and the objects. They cut out the objects and use Scotch tape on one back edge of each to attach it face down on the scene, wherever they choose, so that the objects are not visible but the pictures can be viewed when lifted.

- Students work in pairs, A and B. Student A asks Student B about his/her own picture saying, e.g., *Where are the pencil and book?* Student B lifts a flap and says *They're here* or *They aren't here* depending on where they have stuck their pictures.

- *Optional follow-up activity:* Use toy flashcards. One student leaves the room or closes his/her eyes while you place the flashcard somewhere around the room (partly visible). He/She has to then find it. As a clue, you and the rest of the students name the object repeatedly, speaking more loudly as the student approaches the flashcard and more quietly as he/she moves away.

Extension worksheet 2

- Students cut out the frames from the story and place them on a long strip of paper in the order they remember. Students listen to the story (Track 16) and check their answers. Finally, students stick the frames onto the strip in the correct order and color them in.

Key: 1 F, 2 E, 3 A, 4 C, 5 D, 6 B.

- *Optional follow-up activity:* Say a line from the story to the class. Ask *Monty? Marie? Maskman?* The first student to raise their hand and say which character says the line takes the next turn to say a line.

Song worksheet

- Students color the pictures and cut out the two strips. Help them to cut out the shaded areas in the bottom strip then fold along the lines. They insert the strip with the toys (from the left) and ask, e.g., *Where's my car?* They push the strip to reveal the car and answer *It's here! It's here!* Play the song (Track 17). Students sing while they do this again to reveal the doll and the kite.

- *Optional follow-up activity:* Divide the class into two teams. Show students the toy flashcards before fixing them face down on the board. Ask *Where's the robot?* A student from each team touches the flashcard and says *It's here!* Turn it over to check. Continue with the other toys.

Unit 4 Reinforcement worksheet 1

Follow the lines and color.

Unit 4 — Reinforcement worksheet 2

Make, play, and color.

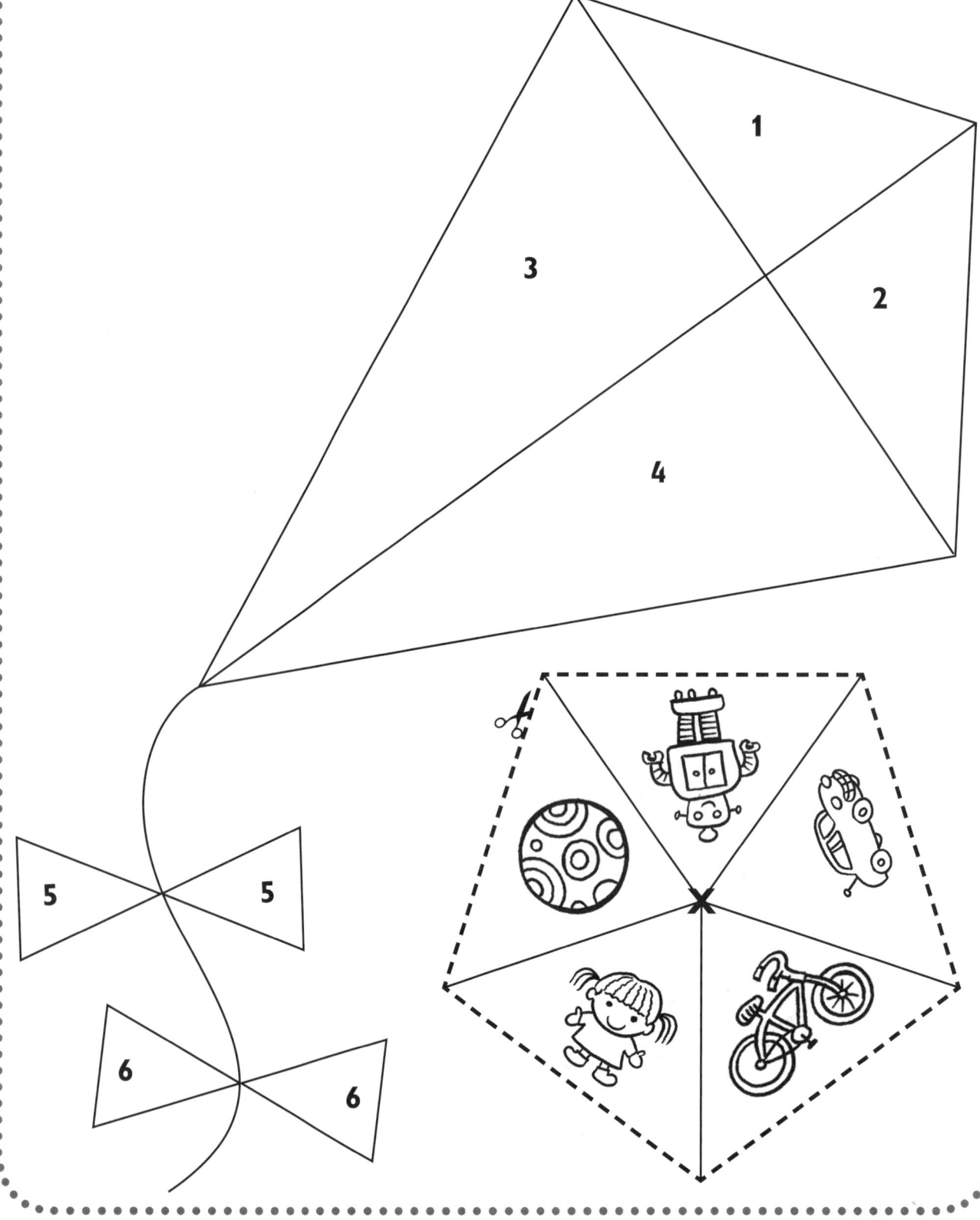

Unit 4 Extension worksheet 1

 Cut, place, and play.

Unit 4 Extension worksheet 2

  Cut and order. Listen.

Song worksheet

 Make and play. Sing.

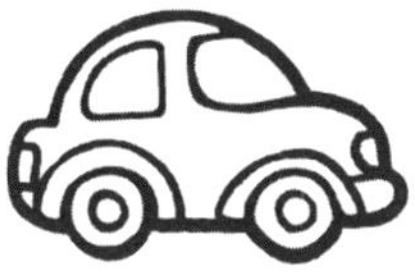

5 Teacher's notes

Reinforcement worksheet 1

- Students look at the pictures and decide (from what each character is wearing and holding) which each character's favorite room is. Explain that the boy in the bathrobe likes the bathroom. Students draw lines between the characters and the rooms. Ask students to circle the bed in the bedroom, the couch in the living room, and the door in the kitchen. Then they color the pictures.

- *Optional follow-up activity:* Students work in small groups and play *Beetles*. Show students a die and draw each face of the die on the board. Next to each face draw the following pictures: 6 – house, 5 – roof, 4 – door, 3 – window, 2 – chimney, 1 – smoke. Students take turns rolling the die and drawing that part of the house. They cannot start until they have rolled a six (the chimney needs a roof first, and the smoke needs a chimney first). There are two windows. If a student rolls a number of a part already drawn (except for the second window), play passes to the next player. The winner is the first to finish the house.

- *Optional audio activity:* Alternatively, students listen to the audio (Track 18). They draw lines between the rooms and the characters. They then color the picture.

Key: bathroom, bedroom, kitchen, living room.

Reinforcement worksheet 2

- Students look at the outline of the house and decide how many of each room they would like in it (maximum of six). They write the numbers in the boxes, and then they design their houses with the number of rooms they have chosen. They decide how many couches and beds to put in. Finally, students color their pictures.

- Students work in pairs, A and B. They hide their pictures from each other and try to guess how many of each room their partner has drawn. Student A names a room, and Student B guesses the number. If he/she is right, Student A says *Yes*, if wrong, *No*. Students A and B exchange roles.

- *Optional follow-up activity:* Copy students' pictures and make them into books. Ask students to flick through the books and decide on a favorite house. The fastest finishers can design the book covers.

- *Optional audio activity:* Alternatively, students listen to the audio (Track 19) and copy the number of rooms into the boxes. They then design their own houses.

Key: 3 bathrooms, 4 bedrooms, 1 kitchen, 2 living rooms.

Extension worksheet 1

- Students look at the pictograms and figure out the meaning of each. They then combine them into sentences and draw the object or character in the correct place.

- Students look at the remaining four objects and choose where to draw them. Students work in pairs, A and B. They take turns describing where they have drawn the objects.

Key: 1 Maskman in bed in bedroom, 2 book on table in kitchen, 3 Monty under chair in living room.

- *Optional follow-up activity:* Students do a survey to find out which are the most popular hiding places. They ask each other, e.g., *Where's the pencil?* and record how many times each room has been chosen.

Extension worksheet 2

- Students look at the pictures. They listen to the story frame by frame (Track 20) and point to the picture that goes with it. As they hear each frame, students write the number in the correct picture. Play the audio again so they can follow the story.

Key: 6, 1, 5, 4, 2, 3.

- *Optional follow-up activity:* Students can use the characters from Reinforcement worksheet 1, Unit 1. Students work in groups of three. Each member of the group has one of the three characters. Play the story. Students lift their character when he or she speaks.

Song worksheet

- Students cut out the three dolls at the bottom of the page. They remember the song and place the dolls in the correct places in the scene. They sing the song (Track 21) and check their answers.

Key: Male doll 1 on the door, Female doll in the bag, Male doll 2 under the bed.

- *Optional follow-up activity:* Students work in pairs, A and B. Together, they think of a name for each doll. Student A says, e.g., *Nessie is under the bed,* and Student B places *Nessie* under the bed. Students A and B exchange roles.

Unit 5 Reinforcement worksheet 1

   Match, color, and circle.

Unit 5 Reinforcement worksheet 2

Think and draw.

Unit 5

Extension worksheet 1

 🔍 ✏️ Look, think, and draw.

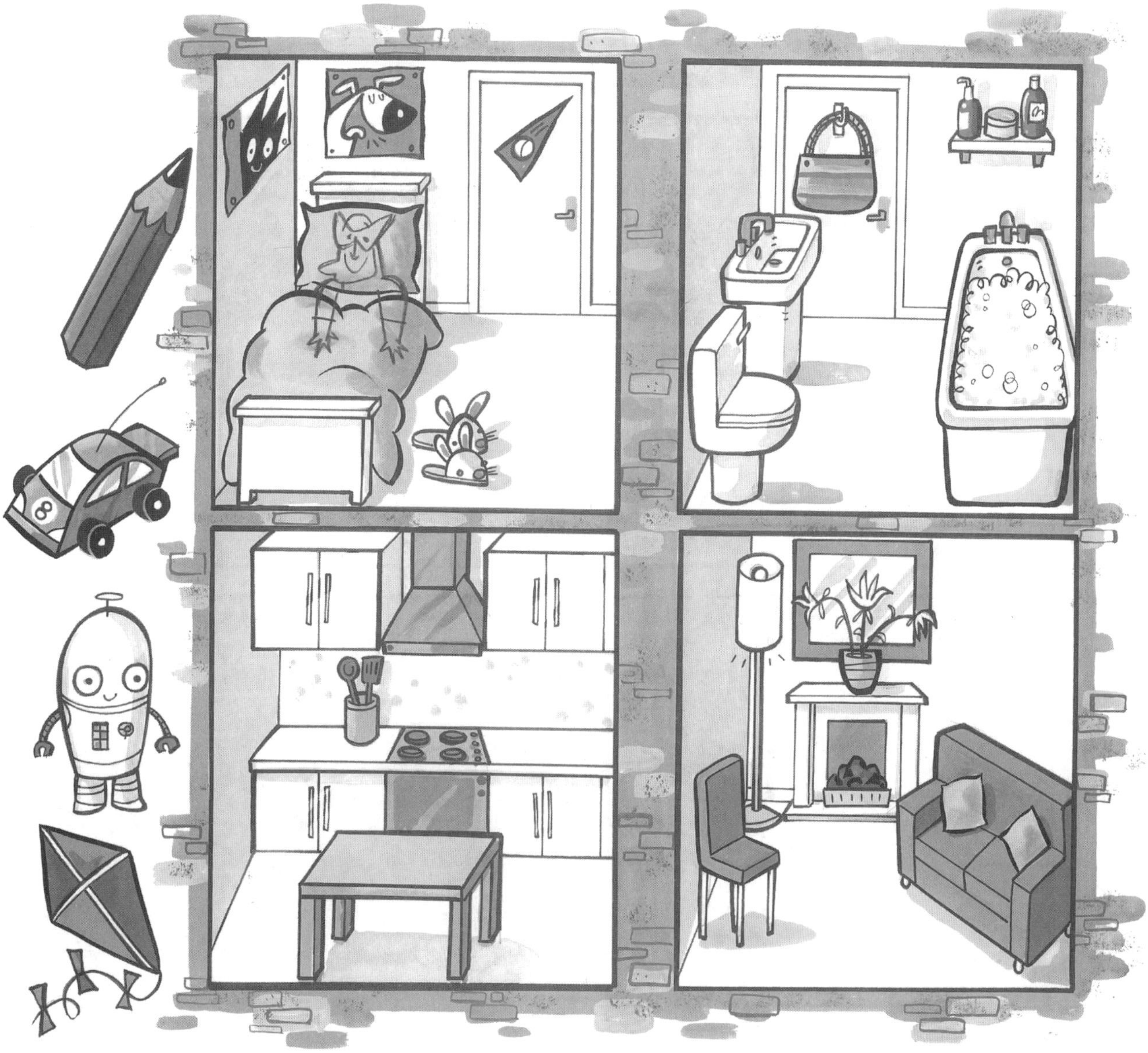

Unit 5

Extension worksheet 2

  Listen, point, and write.

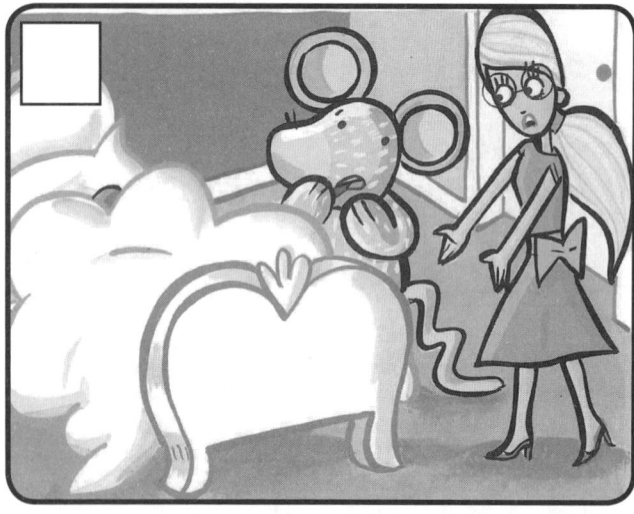

 Unit 5

Song worksheet

 🔊 🎵 Cut and place. Sing.

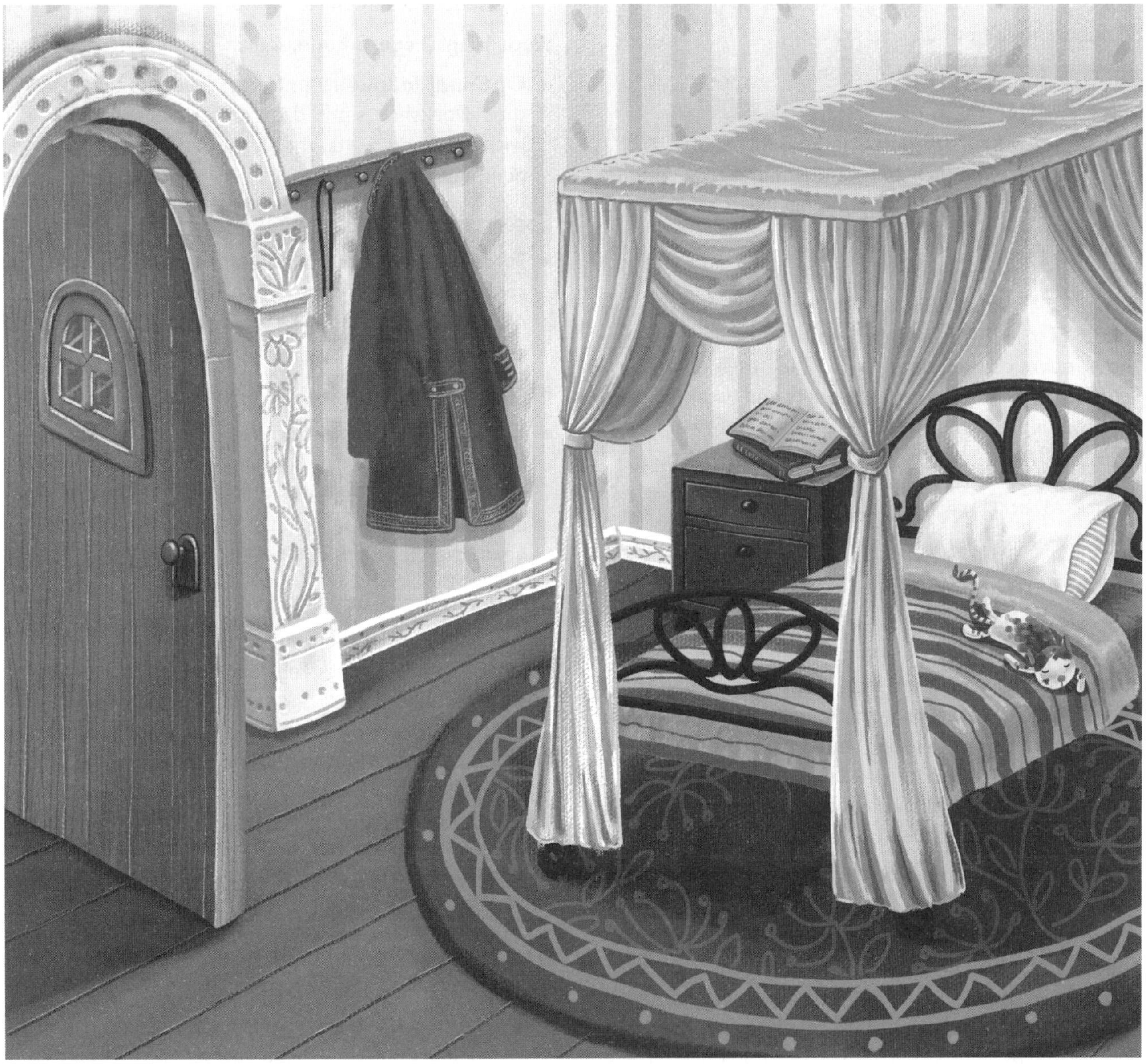

6 Teacher's notes

Reinforcement worksheet 1

- Students look at the pictures at the top of the page. Say a body part, e.g., *mouth*. Students point to the correct row. Students color and cut out the pictures below to make playing cards. They then match the cards to form the four characters: boy, girl, robot, and monster. Ask students to tell you which numbers make up the characters.

  Key: boy: 1, 4, 3; girl: 2, 3, 1; monster: 3, 1, 2; robot: 4, 2, 4.

- *Optional follow-up activity:* Students shuffle the head cards and lay them face down in a row. They do the same with the body and leg cards and then play pelmanism, turning over one card from each row to create a character.

- *Optional audio activity:* Alternatively, play the audio (Track 22). Students point to the different body parts as they are named. They then color, cut out, and match the body parts and listen to the second audio (Track 23) to check their answers.

  Key: Track 22: head, eyes, mouth, legs, arms, hands.
  Track 23: boy: 1, 4, 3; girl: 2, 3, 1; monster: 3, 1, 2; robot: 4, 2, 4.

Reinforcement worksheet 2

- Show students the picture and pre-teach *body*. Students color the body parts in the picture. They use a different color for each body part. When they have finished, students work in pairs, A and B. They guess the colors the other student has used. Student A says, e.g., *Arm number 1 is blue* (or *blue and yellow*). Student B replies *yes* or *no* depending on the color they have chosen. Student A carries on guessing until they have the correct answers. Students then swap roles.

- *Optional follow-up activity:* Students cut out the body parts. Give them round head fasteners and show them how to push them through the crosses to make an articulated robot. Students can use poster putty instead if necessary. They can use their imagination, e.g., put the head for a leg or an arm for a head! If you prefer, students can make their robots at home and bring them in to show the rest of the class.

- *Optional audio activity:* Alternatively, students listen to the audio (Track 24) and color the different body parts in the picture as they are named. Remind them to color each of the body parts a different color. They then continue with the rest of the activity.

  Key: eyes, hands, mouth, head, legs, arms.

Extension worksheet 1

- Students look at the sequences of pictures and draw the correct final item in each sequence. Work through the example with students, emphasizing the intonation of each word to reinforce the sense of a sequence. When they have finished, students chant the sequences in pairs.

  Key: 1 leg, 2 eye, 3 hand, 4 arm, 5 mouth, 6 head.

- *Optional follow-up activity:* Students turn over their worksheets and draw their own sequences with the body parts, then give them to their partners to complete.

Extension worksheet 2

- Students look at the pictures and decide who is speaking in each frame. They circle the character, *A* or *B*. Students listen to the story (Track 25) and check their answers.

  Key: 1 B, 2 A, 3 A, 4 B, 5 B, 6 A.

- *Optional follow-up activity:* In small groups, Student A says, e.g., *I have an arm … .* Student B says, e.g., *I have an arm and a leg … .* Play continues until all six body parts have been named and the next student starts again.

Song worksheet

- Students look at the body parts and name them (*eyes, arms* and *hands, legs* and *feet, mouths*). They then remember the song and color the alien's body parts orange and the boy's body parts blue. Students compare their answers in pairs, A and B. Student A says e.g., *The alien has three eyes,* and Student B says, *Yes* or *No*. Students A and B exchange roles. They sing the song (Track 26) and check their answers. Students then draw a picture of the two friends (alien and boy) in the frame.

  Key: Alien: 4 arms, 4 hands, 3 eyes, 2 mouths, 6 legs. Boy: 2 arms, 2 hands, 2 eyes, 1 mouth, 2 legs.

- *Optional follow-up activity:* Play *Beetles* in pairs or small groups (see Reinforcement worksheet 1, Unit 5). Use body parts instead of house parts as follows: 6 – body, 5 – head, 4 – arm, 3 – leg, 2 – eye, 1 – mouth. Students add a body part each time they roll a number to make monsters. They cannot start until they roll a 6. They need a head (5) to be able to draw the eye(s) and mouth(s).

Unit 6 Reinforcement worksheet 1

Look, cut, and match.

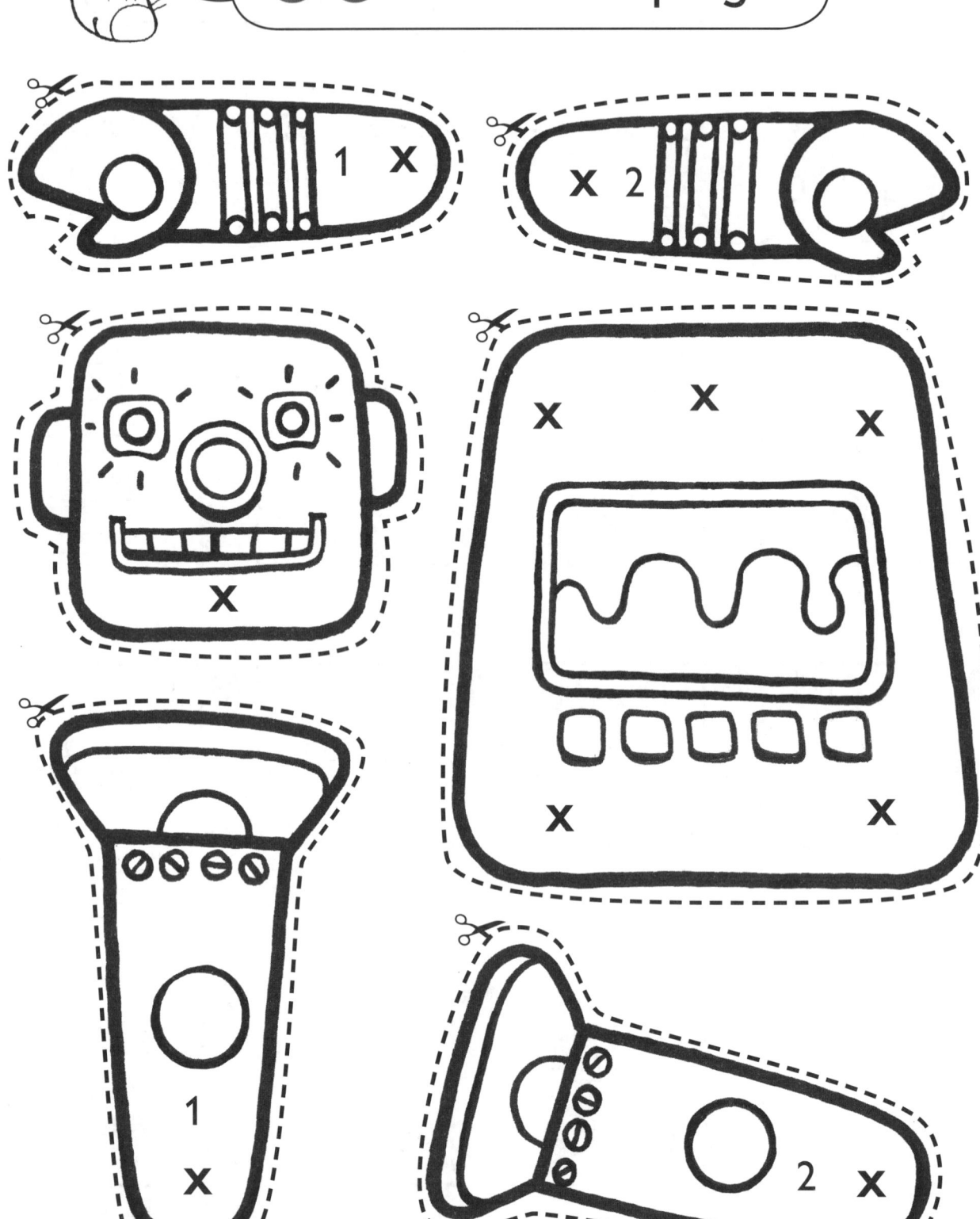

Unit 6 Reinforcement worksheet 2

Color and play.

Unit 6

Extension worksheet 1

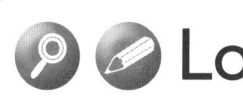

Look and complete.

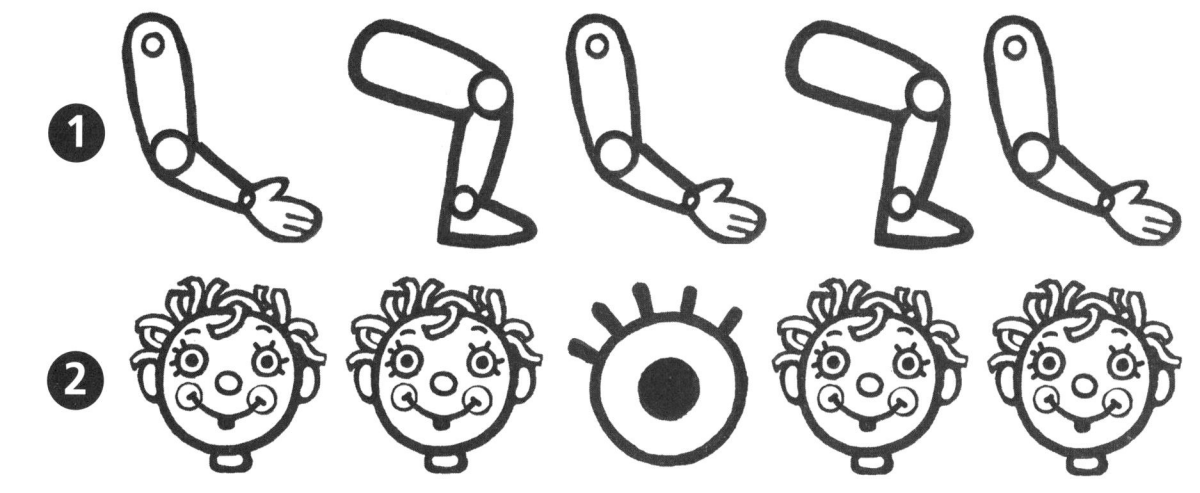

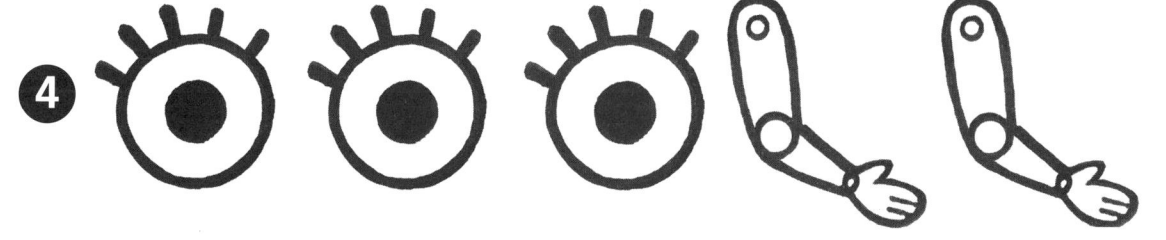

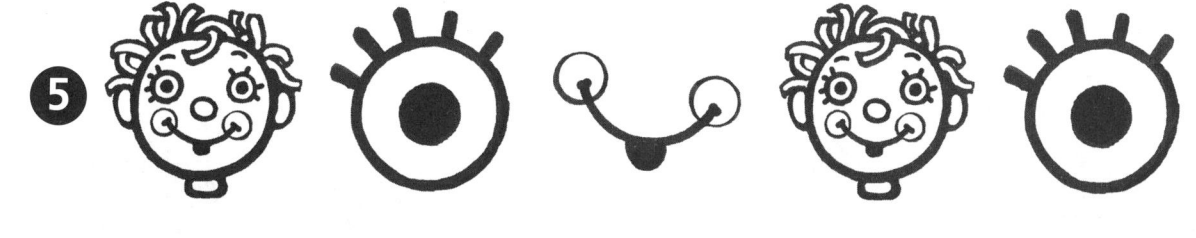

Unit 6

Extension worksheet 2

Look and circle. Listen.

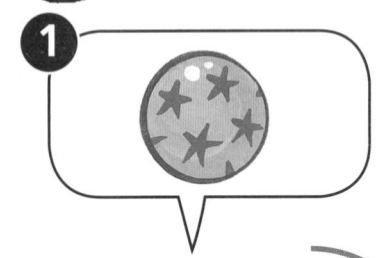

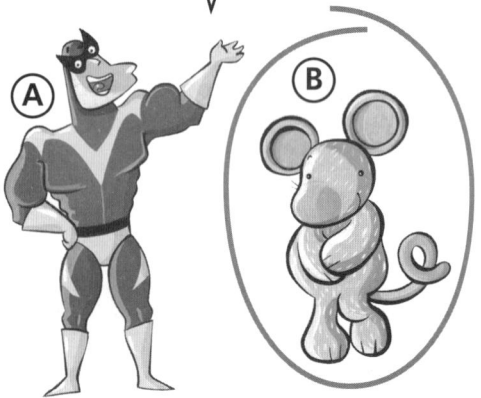

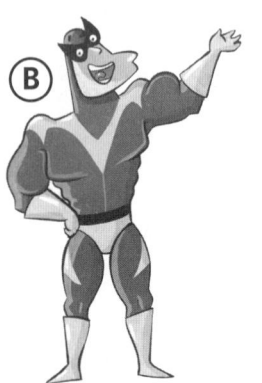

Unit 6 Song worksheet

Color and draw. Sing.

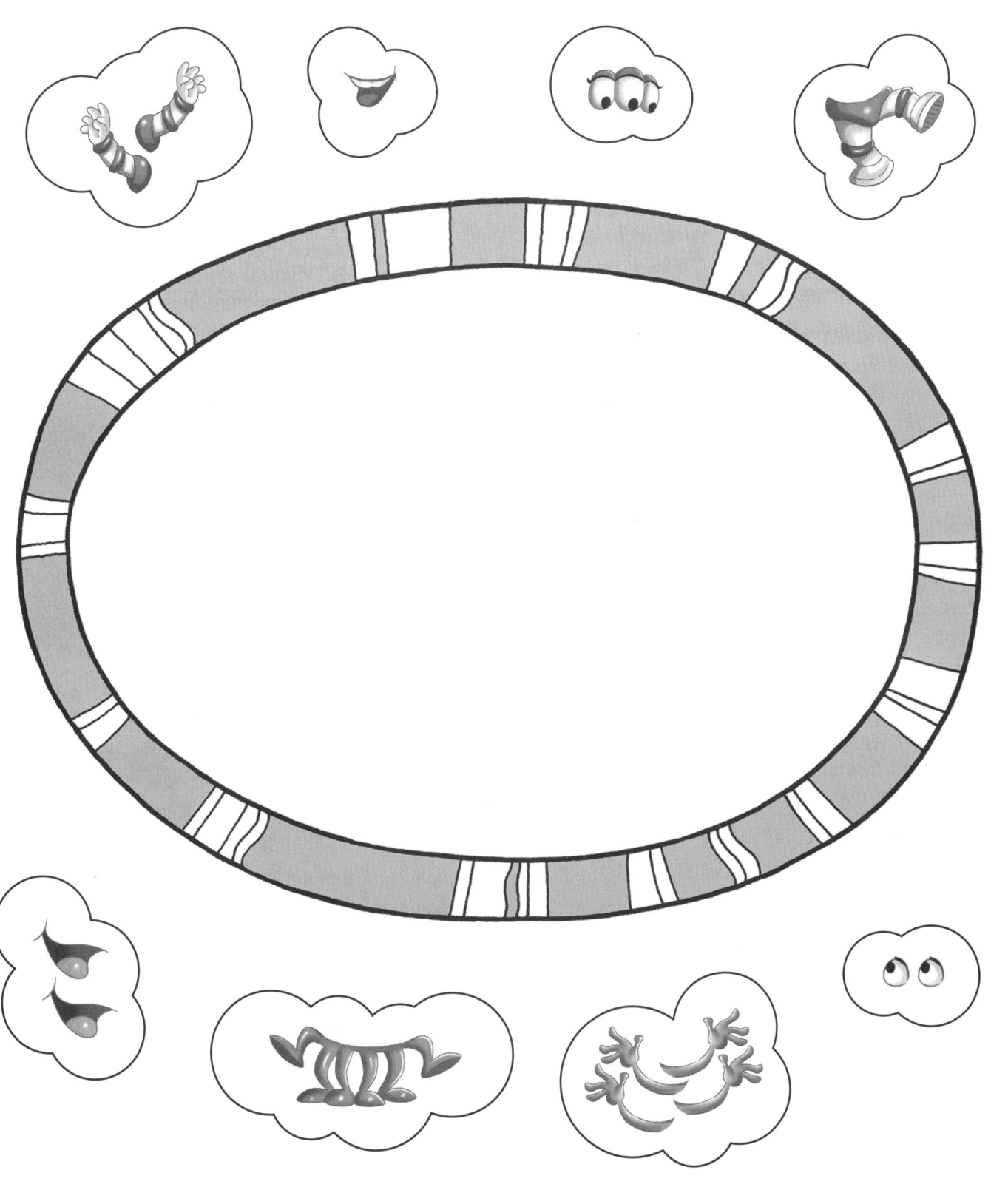

7 Teacher's notes

Reinforcement worksheet 1

- Name an animal (*tiger*, *duck*, *frog*, *dog*, *bird*, or *mouse*) and ask students to point to the correct trail. Students follow the rest of the trails to the hiding places. Students then cut out the animals and stick them in the correct hiding places. Finally, ask students to draw a fish in the pond.

- *Optional follow-up activity:* Students work in pairs, A and B. Student A names an animal, and Student B follows the trail to the hiding place. Students A and B exchange roles.

- *Optional audio activity:* Alternatively, students listen to the audio (Track 27) and follow the trail from the animal to the hiding place. They then continue with the rest of the activity.

Key: tiger, duck, frog, dog, bird, mouse.

Reinforcement worksheet 2

- Ask students to name the animals on the left-hand side and then do a quick survey to see which is the favorite. Say *Hands up if your favorite animal is the tiger!* and do the same with the other animals. Students look at the animal heads and draw lines to match them to their bottom halves.

Key: 1 – 5, 2 – 3, 3 – 4, 4 – 6, 5 – 1, 6 – 2.

- *Optional follow-up activity:* Students fold along the lines (connect *a* to *c*, leaving *b* inside) to create original animals. Check that students know the correct name of each animal, then ask them to create the name for the new, folded animal, e.g., *fish tiger* or *figer*.

- *Optional audio activity:* Alternatively, students listen to the audio (Track 28) and point to the animal heads as they are mentioned. They then draw lines to match them to their bottom halves.

Key: bird: 3 – 4, fish: 1 – 5, mouse: 2 – 3, duck: 4 – 6, dog: 6 – 2, tiger: 5 – 1.

Extension worksheet 1

- Mime the three actions *fly*, *jump*, and *swim* to elicit the vocabulary, then ask students to look at the first row of pictures. Say *A frog **can** swim*, then do the same with *fish* and *duck*. When you say *A doll **can't** swim*, explain that this one is the one that doesn't belong.

- Students work through the rows of pictures and circle the ones that don't belong. To check their answers, students work in pairs and take turns saying what each thing can and can't do.

Key: 1 doll, 2 tiger, 3 kite, 4 dog, 5 kite.

- *Optional follow-up activity:* Divide the class into four groups and give an animal name to each group: *fish*, *frog*, *duck*, and *bird*. Say, e.g., *I can fly*. The students from the *duck* and *bird* teams do the action, e.g., flap their wings. Repeat with the other actions.

Extension worksheet 2

- Students look at the pictures. They circle the character who is speaking about his/her animal in each frame. Students listen to the story (Track 29) and check their answers.

Key: 1 Monty, 2 Monty, 3 Maskman, 4 Maskman, 5 Marie, 6 Marie.

- *Optional follow-up activity:* Shuffle the animal flashcards and hand them face down to one of the students. He/She chooses one of the cards and looks at it without letting the other students see. He/She then mimes the animal and the rest have to guess which animal it is. As they guess, students join in with the mime. The cards are reshuffled, and another student does the mime.

Song worksheet

- Students look at the pictures and the actions and complete the chart by circling the correct action for each animal. They sing the song (Track 30) and check their answers. In pairs, they take turns interpreting the chart, e.g., *A frog can jump and swim, but it can't fly.*

Key:

- *Optional follow-up activity:* Students make pictures. They color and cut out the animals next to the chart and stick them to the scene.

42

Unit 7

Reinforcement worksheet 1

🔍 ▶ Look and place the animals.

Unit 7 Reinforcement worksheet 2

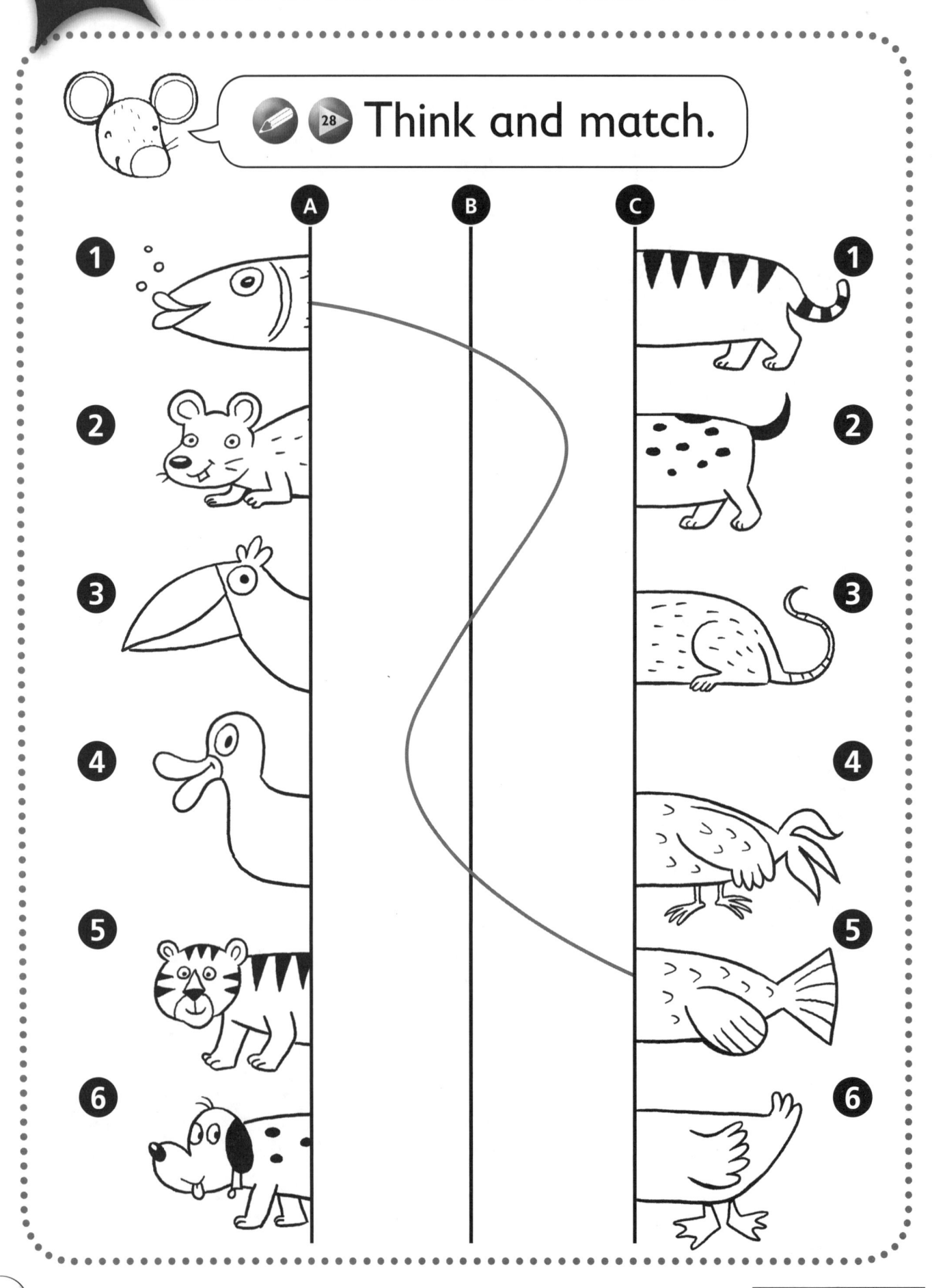

Think and match.

Unit 7

Extension worksheet 1

🔍 ✏️ Look, think, and circle.

1. 
2. 
3. 
4. 
5.

Unit 7

Extension worksheet 2

✏️ 🔊 Look and circle. Listen.

Unit 7

Song worksheet

🎵 Think and circle. Sing.

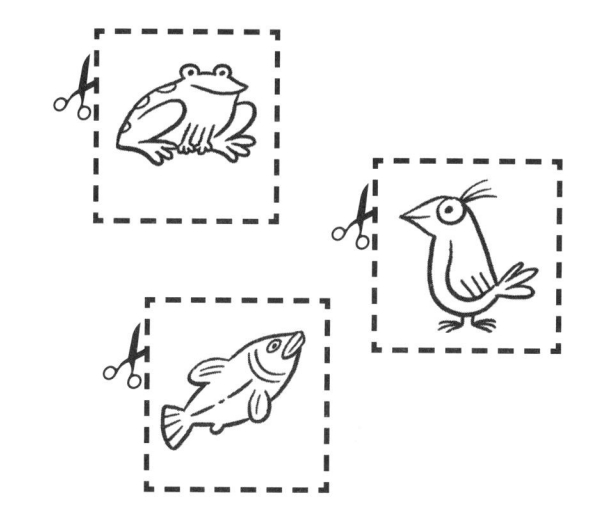

8 Teacher's notes

Reinforcement worksheet 1

- Students connect the dots to draw the foods. When they have finished, they rank each food with an emoticon in the circle next to each picture, e.g., happy face: ☺ if they really like the food, straight face: 😐 if they think it is OK, and sad face: ☹ if they don't like it. In groups, or as a class, students find out which are the most and least popular foods. Name a food and ask the students with happy faces to raise their hands, then do the same with the other faces.

- *Optional follow-up activity:* Use food flashcards. Students sit in a circle. Give one student a flashcard and ask them to pass it around the circle as you say the unit chant. The student who has the flashcard as you finish the chant names it. Continue with the remaining flashcards.

- *Optional audio activity:* Alternatively, students look at the incomplete pictures and connect the dots. They then listen to the audio (Track 31). When they hear the food, they point to the correct picture. Then they draw a happy or sad face next to each food to show whether they like or don't like it.

Key: fruit, milk, cake, tomato, eggs, fries.

Reinforcement worksheet 2

- Students point to the different foods as you name them. Students then use a pencil to follow the lines between the foods at the top and the bottom of the page. Finally, they color the foods, using the same colors for each pair.

- *Optional follow-up activity:* Students work in groups of three. One student names a food, and the other two have to point to that food at the top of the page. They then race each other, following the spaghetti line, to the same food at the bottom of the page.

- *Optional audio activity:* Alternatively, students point to the food and follow the spaghetti lines as they listen to the audio (Track 32). They then color the food.

Key: fries, tomato, milk, fruit, cake, egg.

Extension worksheet 1

- Use one worksheet per group or play as a class. The first student names a food, e.g., *eggs,* and the student on his/her left says *I like eggs* or *I don't like eggs.* If the answer is *I like,* the first student colors in a section of the chart next to the correct picture. Students continue to ask around the group until the pie chart is complete and they can see which the favorite food is.

- *Optional follow-up activity:* Fix the food flashcards to the board and draw a happy face and a sad face underneath each one. Two students come to the front. Name a food, e.g., *milk.* The students make a happy face or sad face depending on whether they like or don't like the food. Ask them to say the sentence, for example *I like milk.* Continue with other foods and students.

Extension worksheet 2

- Students cut out the frames from the story and place them on a long strip of paper in the order they remember. Students listen to the story (Track 33) and check their answers. Finally, students stick the frames onto the strip in the correct order and color them in.

Key: 1 B, 2 F, 3 C, 4 E, 5 A, 6 D.

- *Optional follow-up activity:* Say a line from the story to the class. Ask *Monty? Marie? Maskman?* The first student to raise their hand and say which character says the line takes the next turn to say a line.

Song worksheet

- Students look at the two empty plates. Point to the plate with the happy face and say *I like*; then point to the plate with the sad face and say *I don't like.* Students look at the pictograms of the food and draw a line between the food and the plate, depending on whether the parrot liked or didn't like the food. Students sing the song (Track 34) and check their answers.

Key: Like: tomatoes, fruit, cake, milk.
Don't like: fries, eggs.

- *Optional follow-up activity:* Put the six food flashcards on the floor and place an empty plastic bottle on top of each. Give one student a ball and ask him/her to roll it toward the bottles. When he/she knocks down a bottle, he/she has to say whether he/she likes or doesn't like that food.

Unit 8 — Reinforcement worksheet 1

Think and draw faces.

Unit 8 Reinforcement worksheet 2

Follow the lines and color.

Unit 8 Extension worksheet 1

Ask, answer, and color.

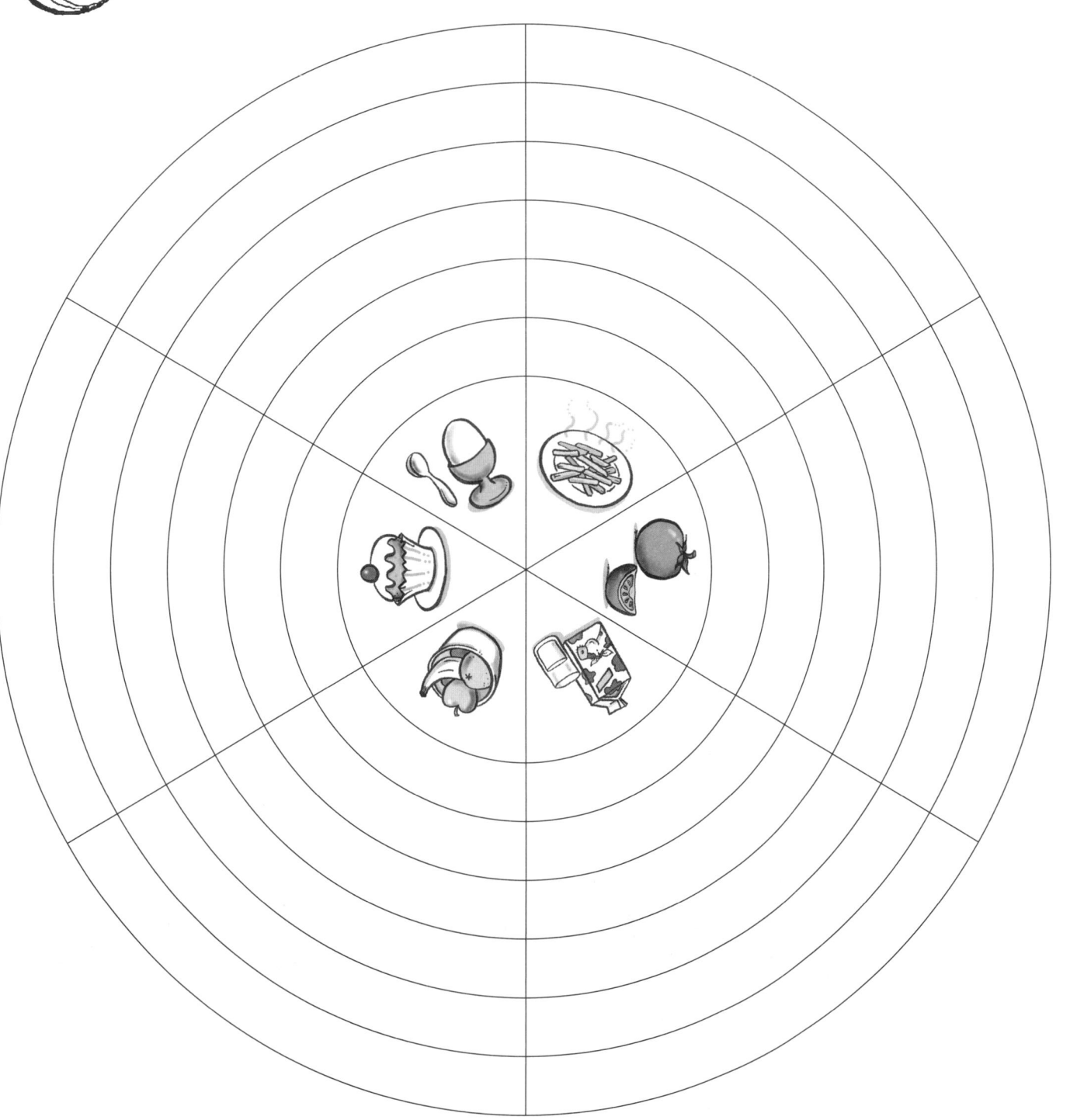

Unit 8

Extension worksheet 2

Cut and order. Listen.

A B C D E F

Unit 8

Song worksheet

Look and match. Sing.

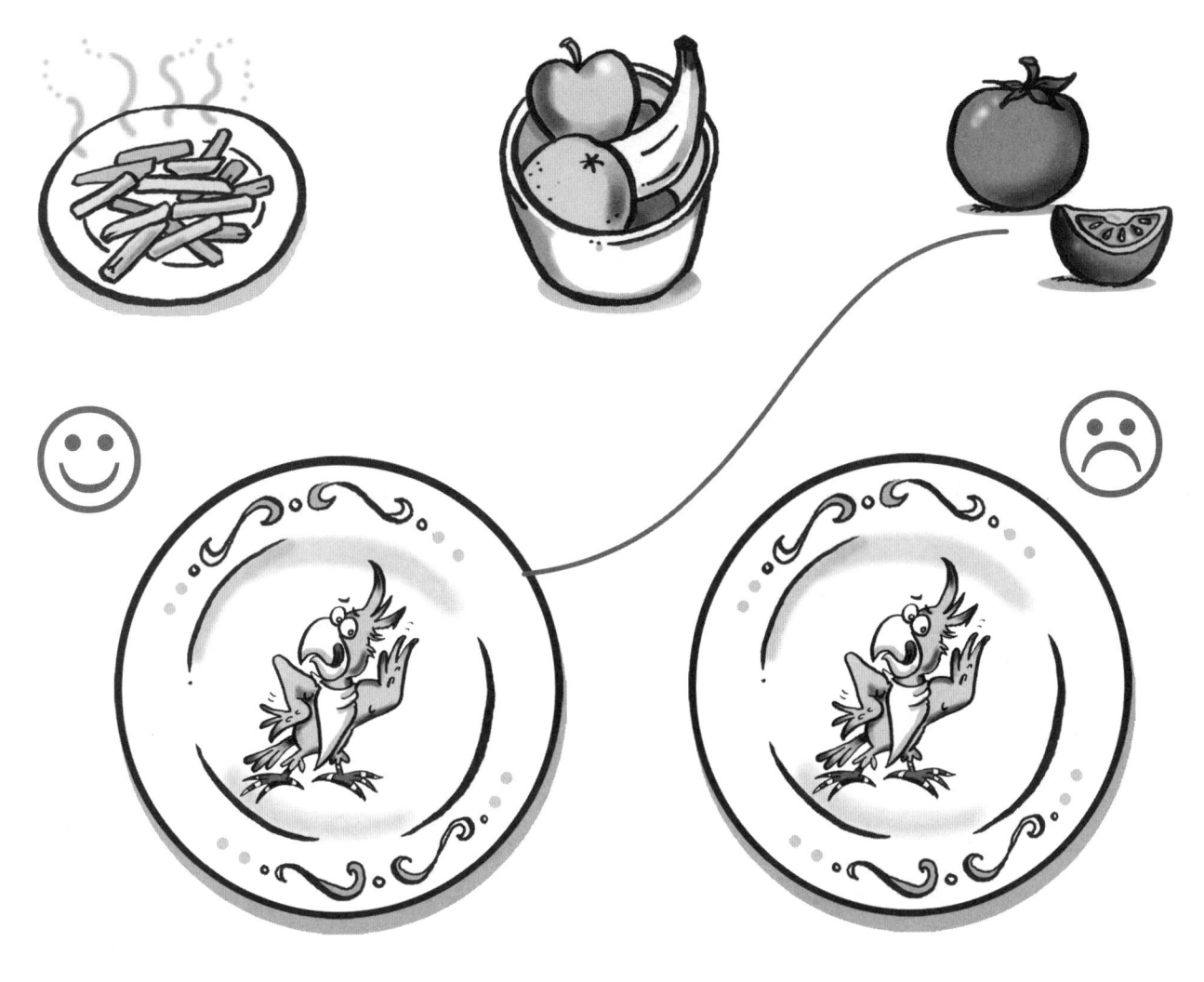

Hi!

Name: _____

Thanks and acknowledgments

Kathryn Escribano wishes to thank the staff and children at the CP Narciso Alonso Cortés, Valladolid (Spain) on whom the ideas have been tried and tested. She would also like to acknowledge the patience and understanding of her family and friends from whom time was taken to write this book.

The authors and publishers are grateful to the following illustrators:

Melanie Sharp, c/o Sylvie Poggio; Gary Swift; Lisa Williams, c/o Sylvie Poggio; Emily Skinner, c/o Graham-Cameron Illustration; Lisa Smith, c/o Sylvie Poggio; Chris Garbutt, c/o Arena.

The publishers are grateful to the following contributors:

Bridget Kelly: editor
Wild Apple Design: book design and page make-up
Lon Chan: cover design
John Green and Tim Woolf, TEFLAudio: audio recordings
Songs written and produced by Robert Lee, Dib Dib Dub Studios
John Marshall Media, Inc. and Lisa Hutchins: audio recordings for the American English edition
hyphen S.A.: publishing management, American English edition